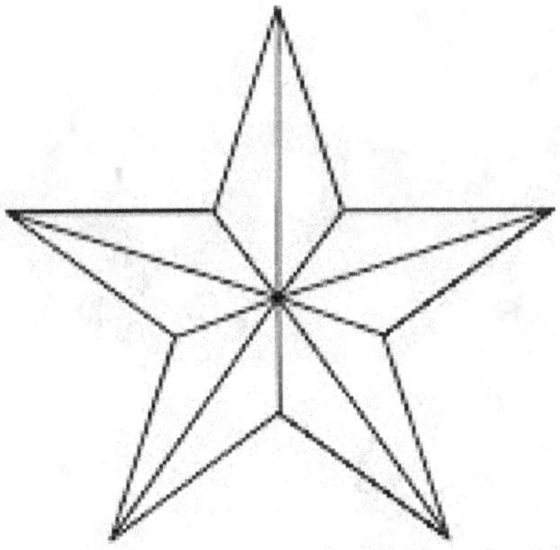

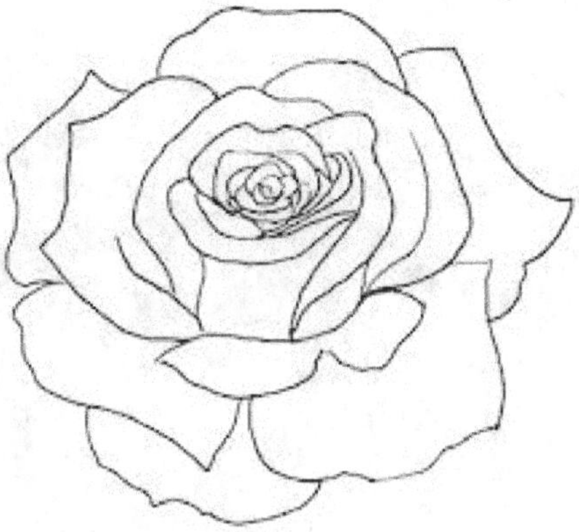

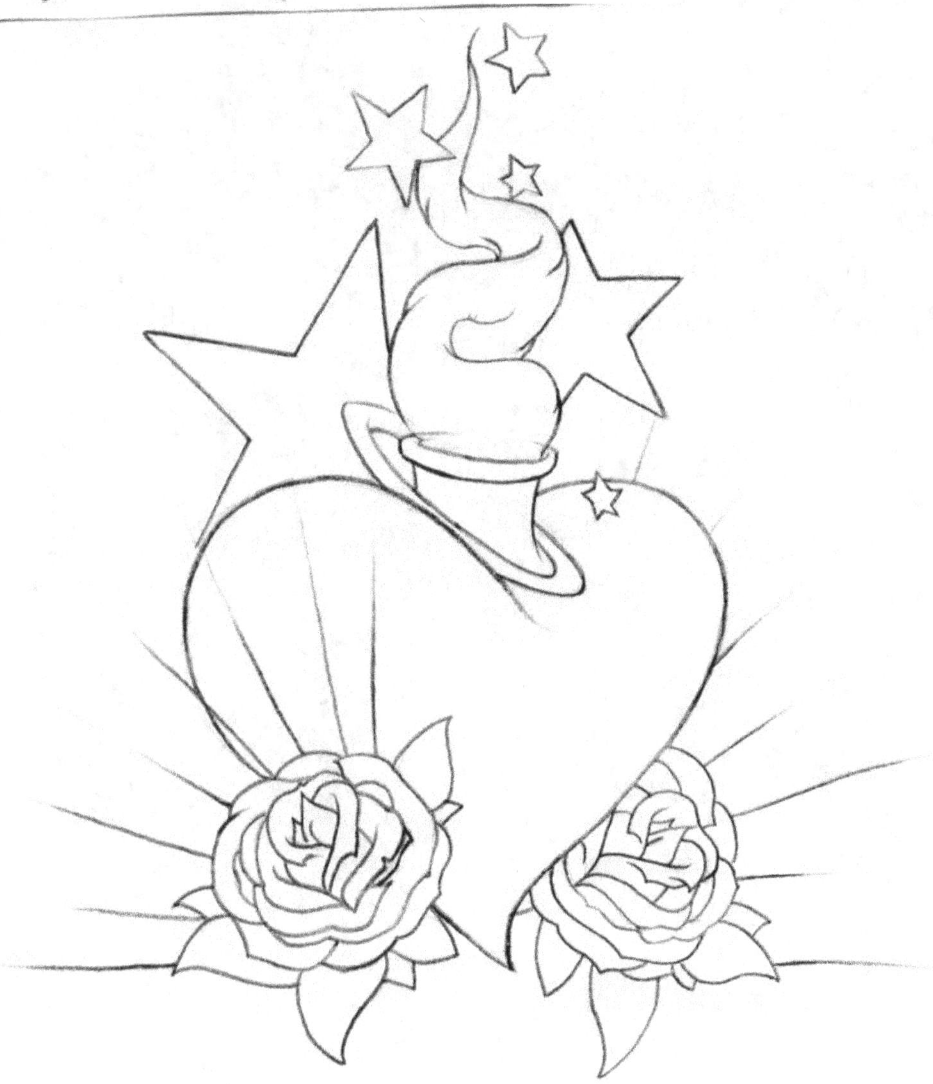

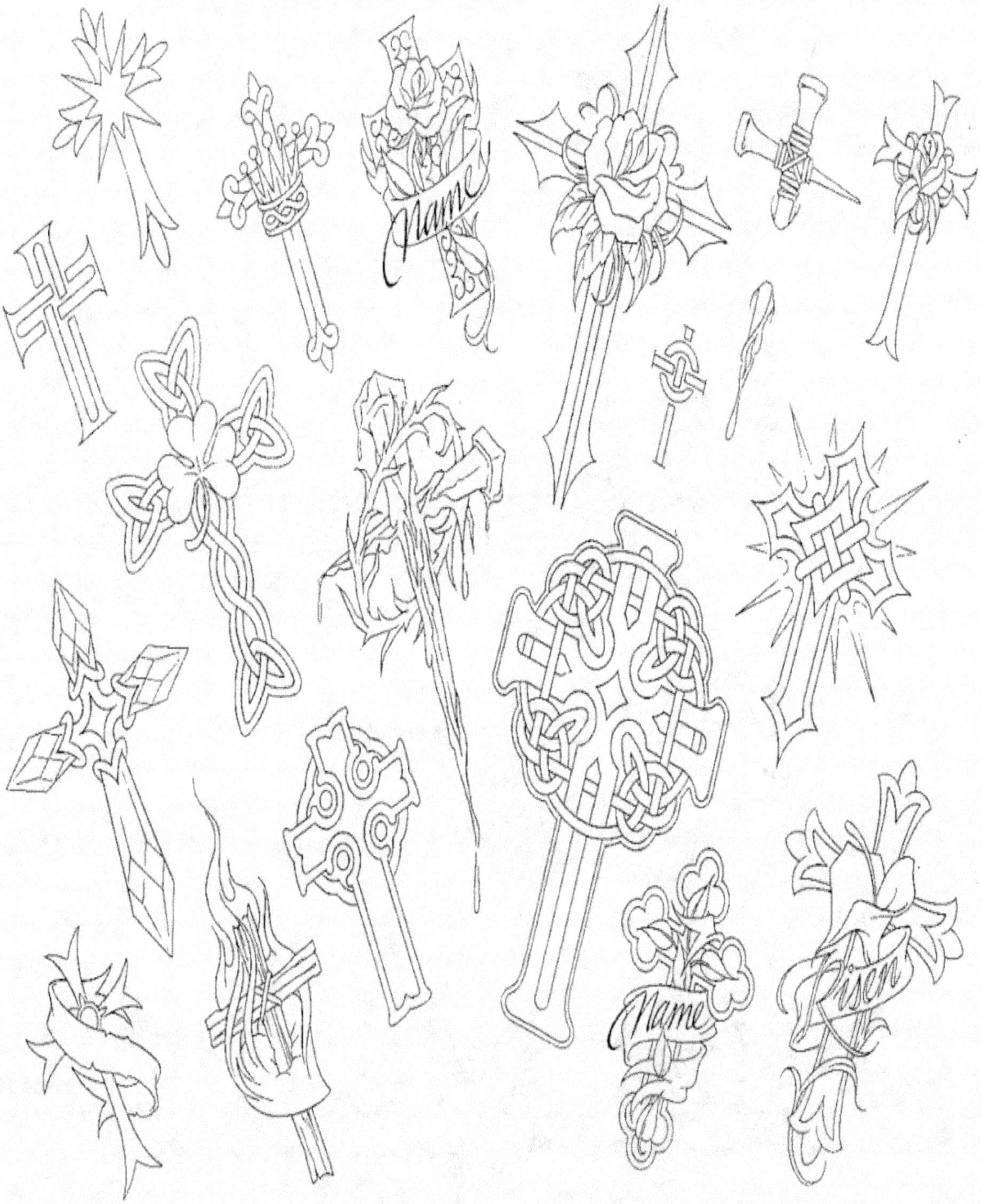
Name
Name
Risen

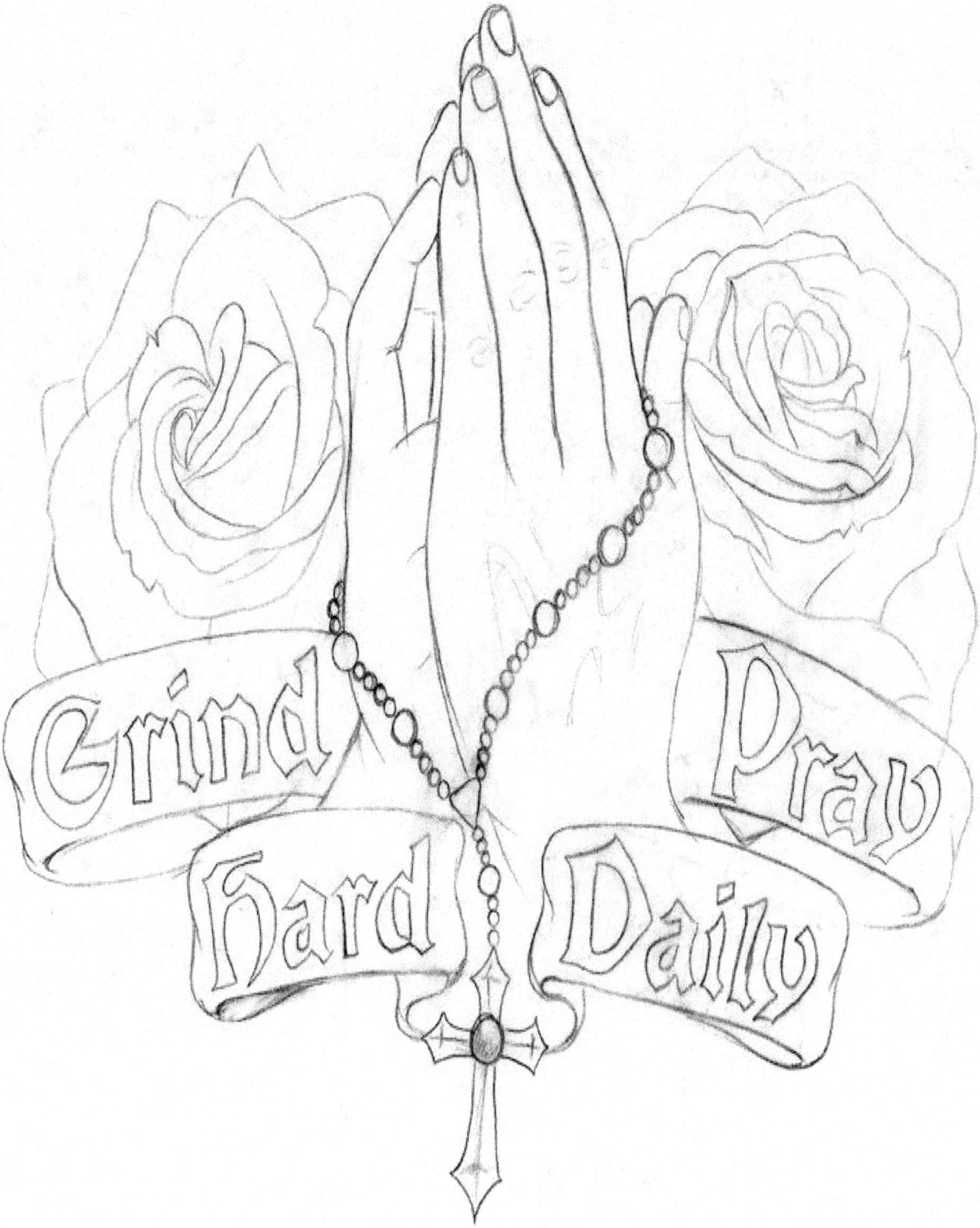
Grind
Hard
Pray
Daily

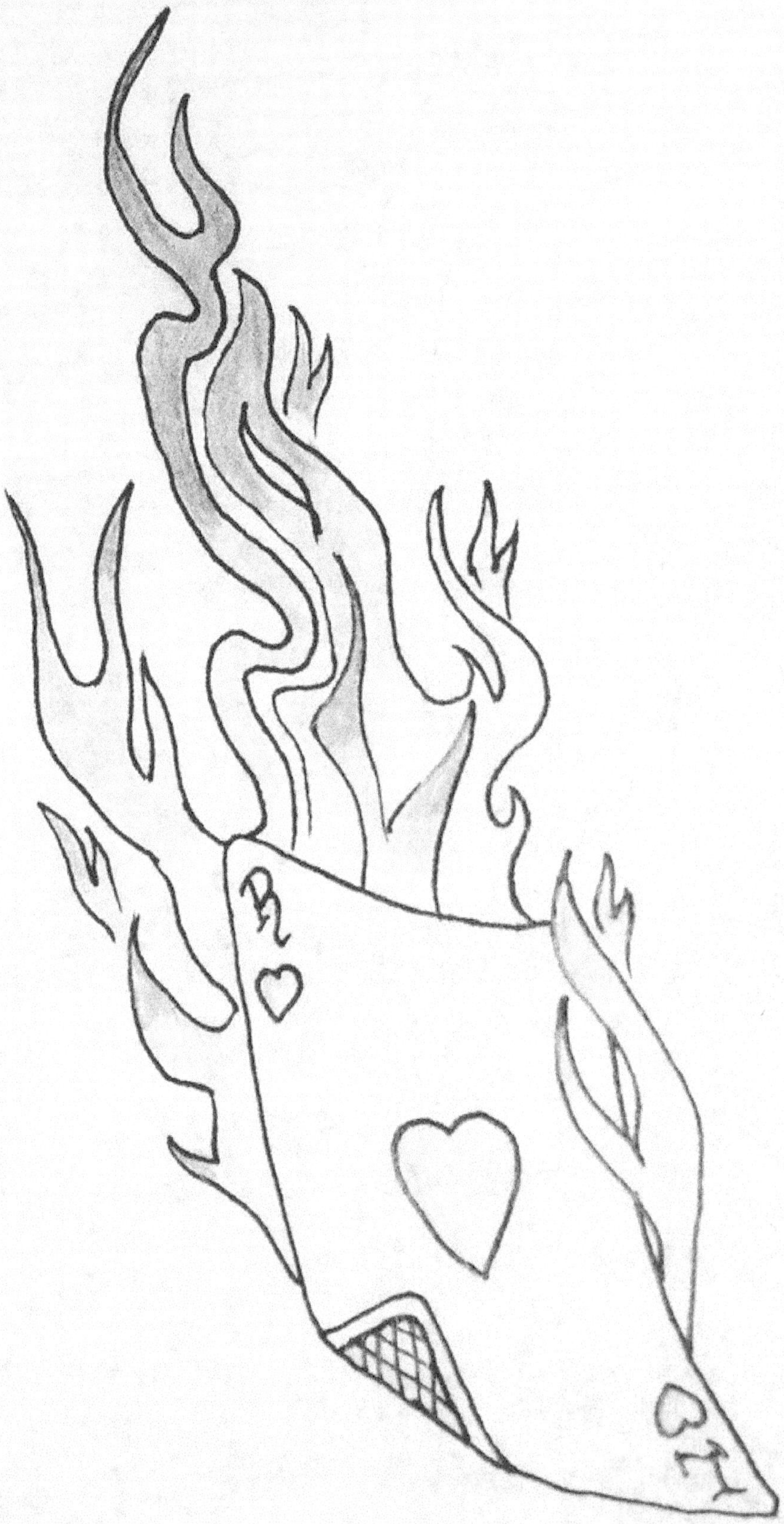

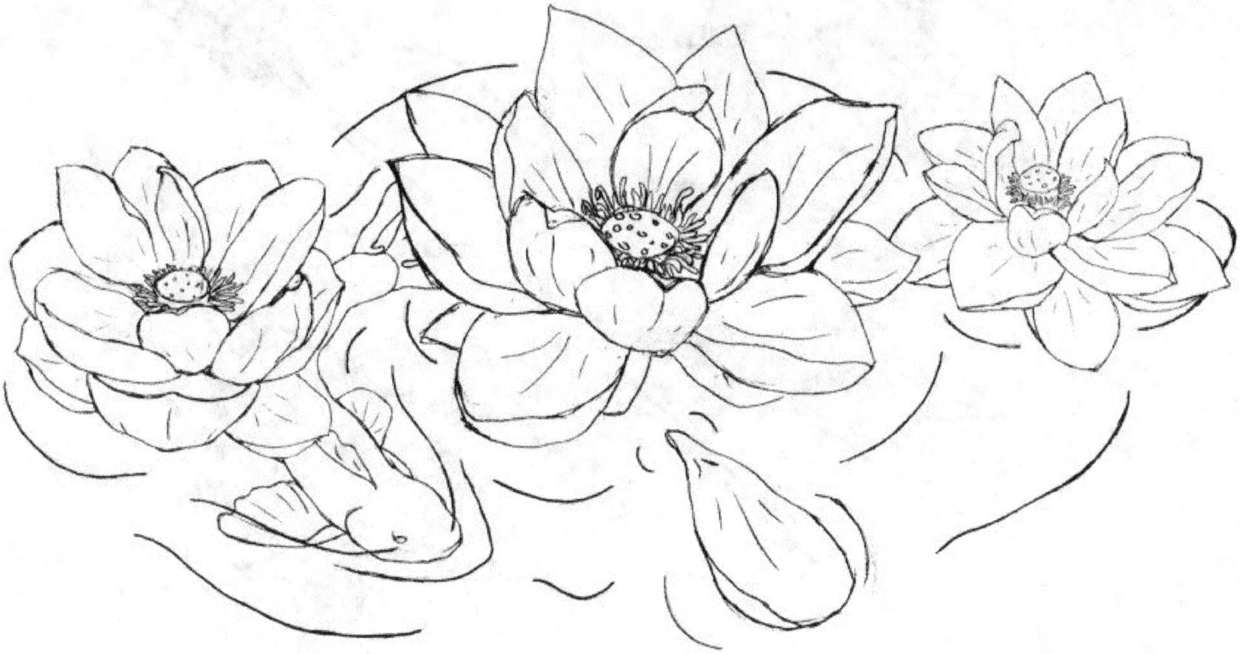

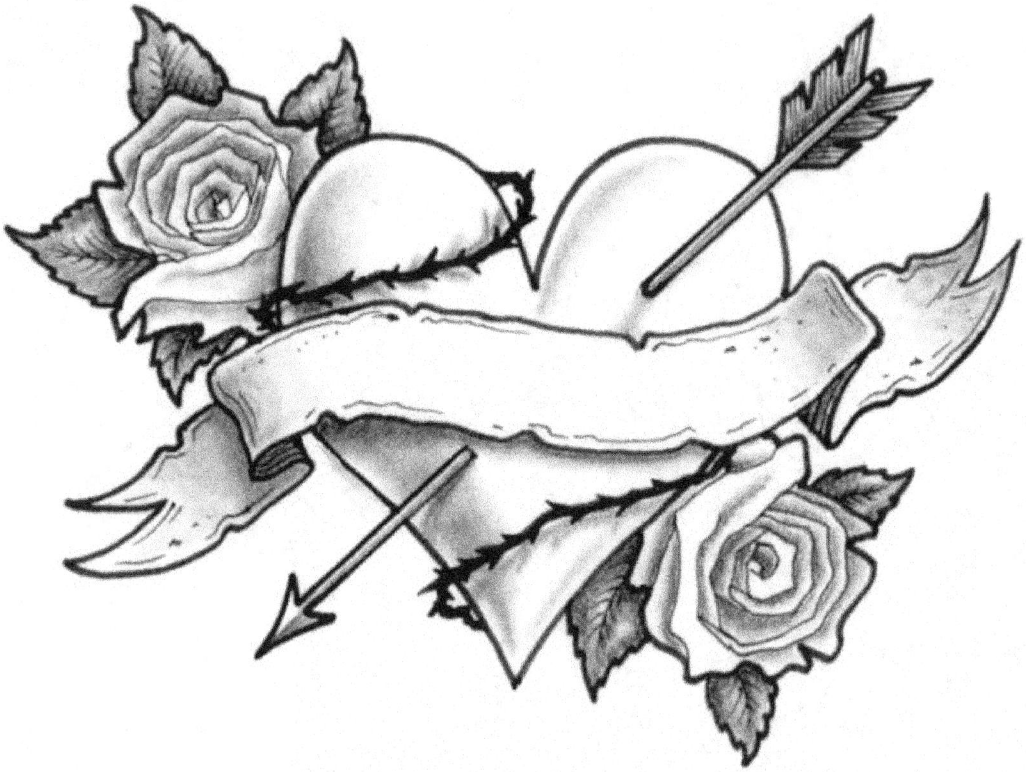

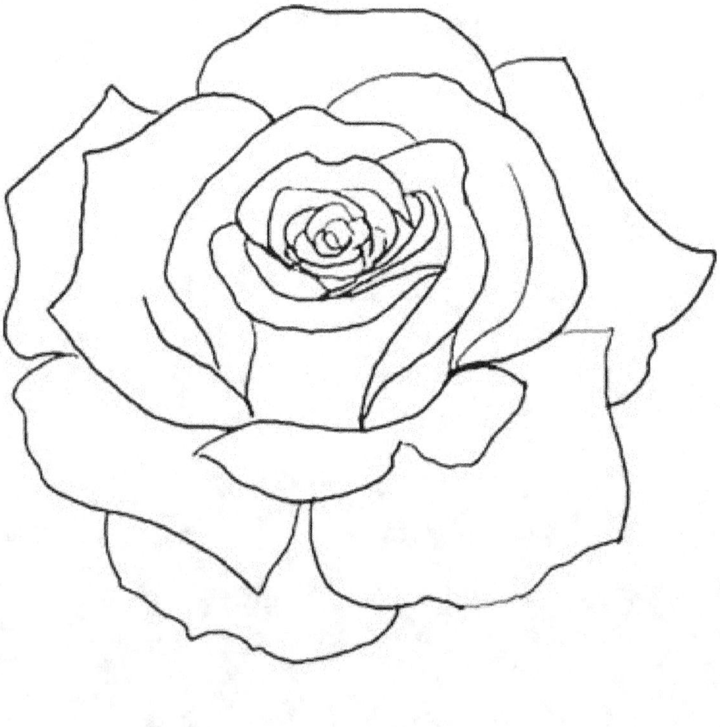

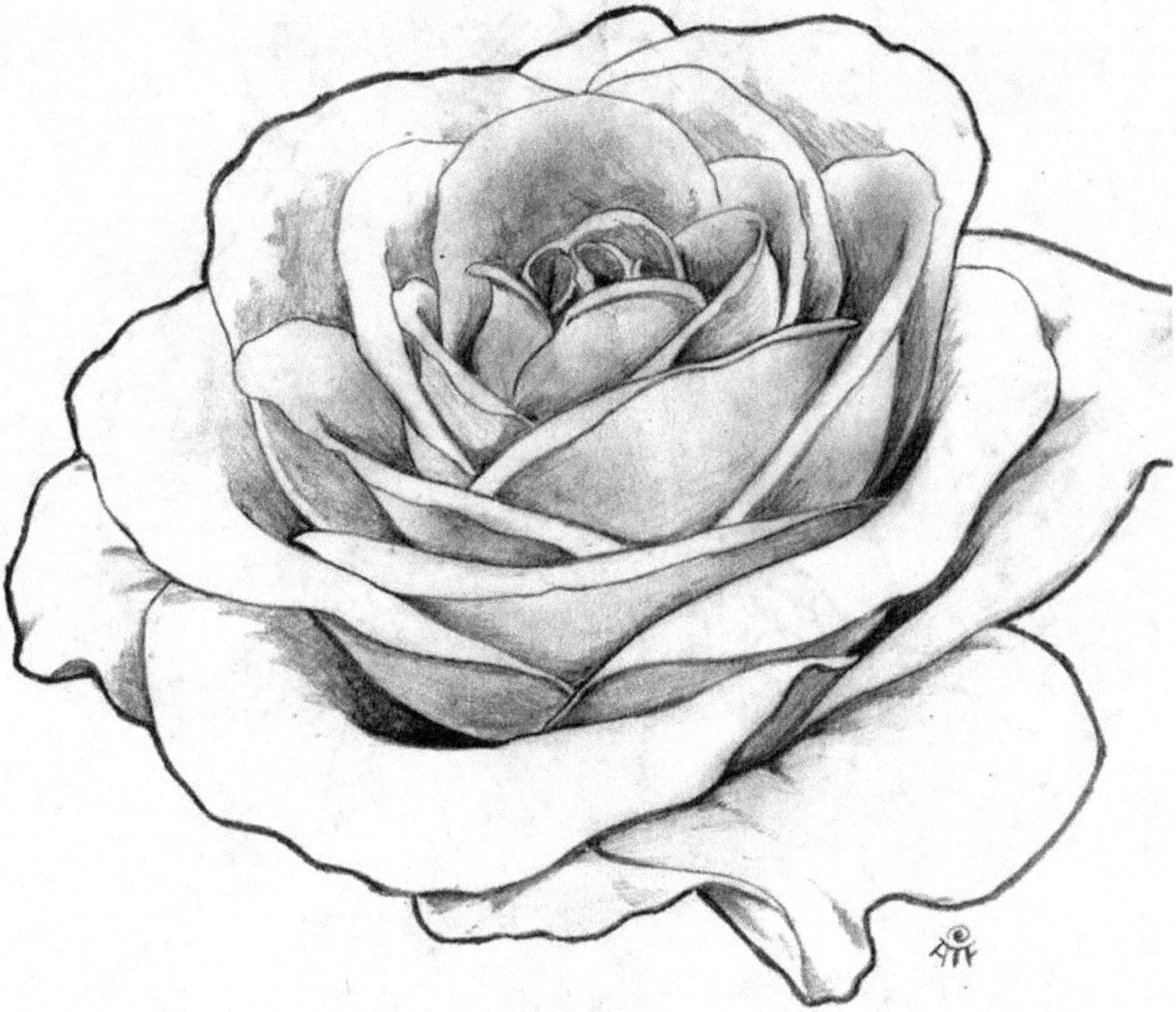

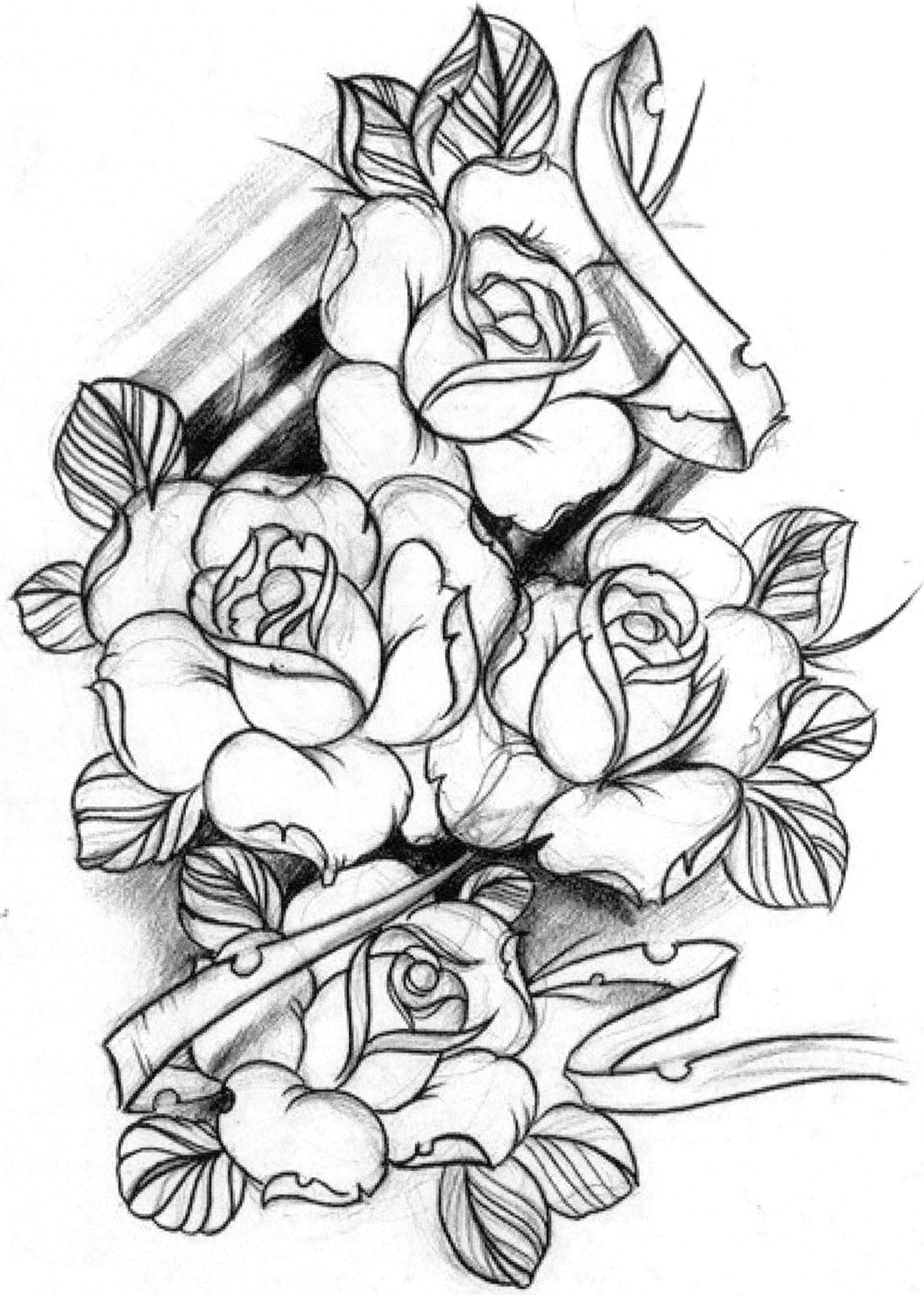

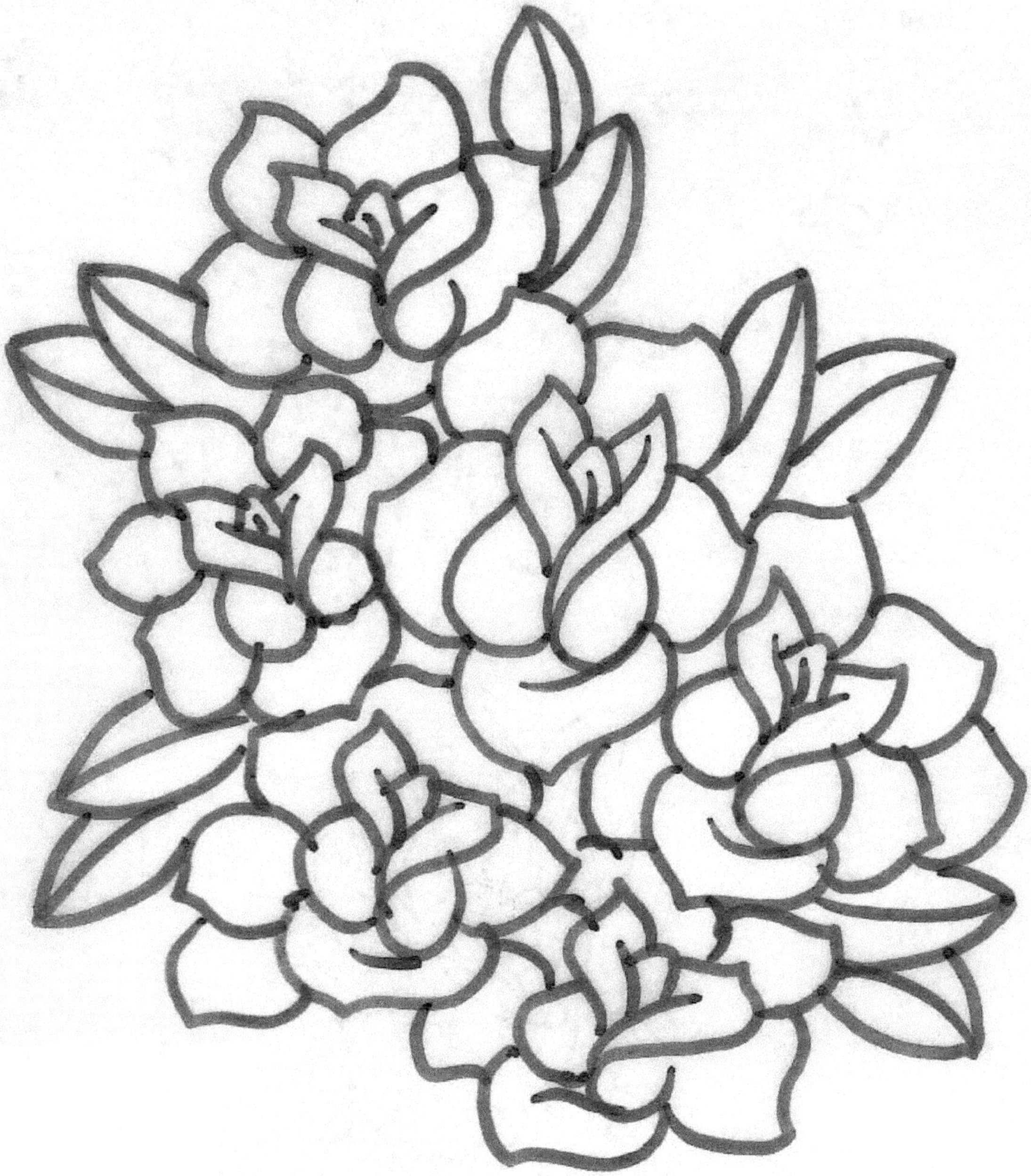

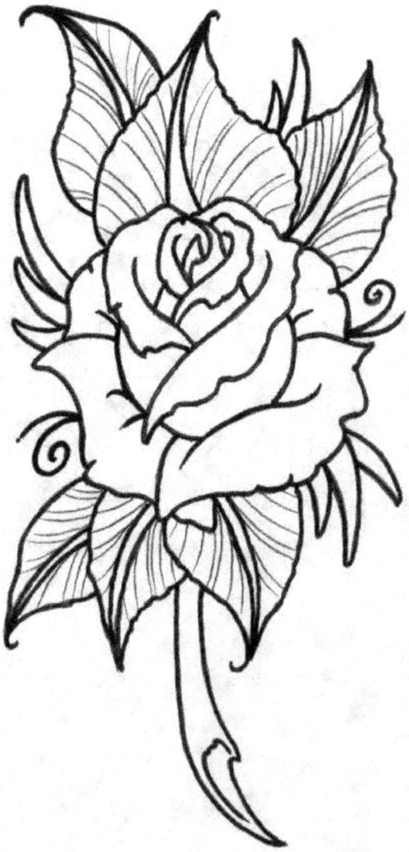

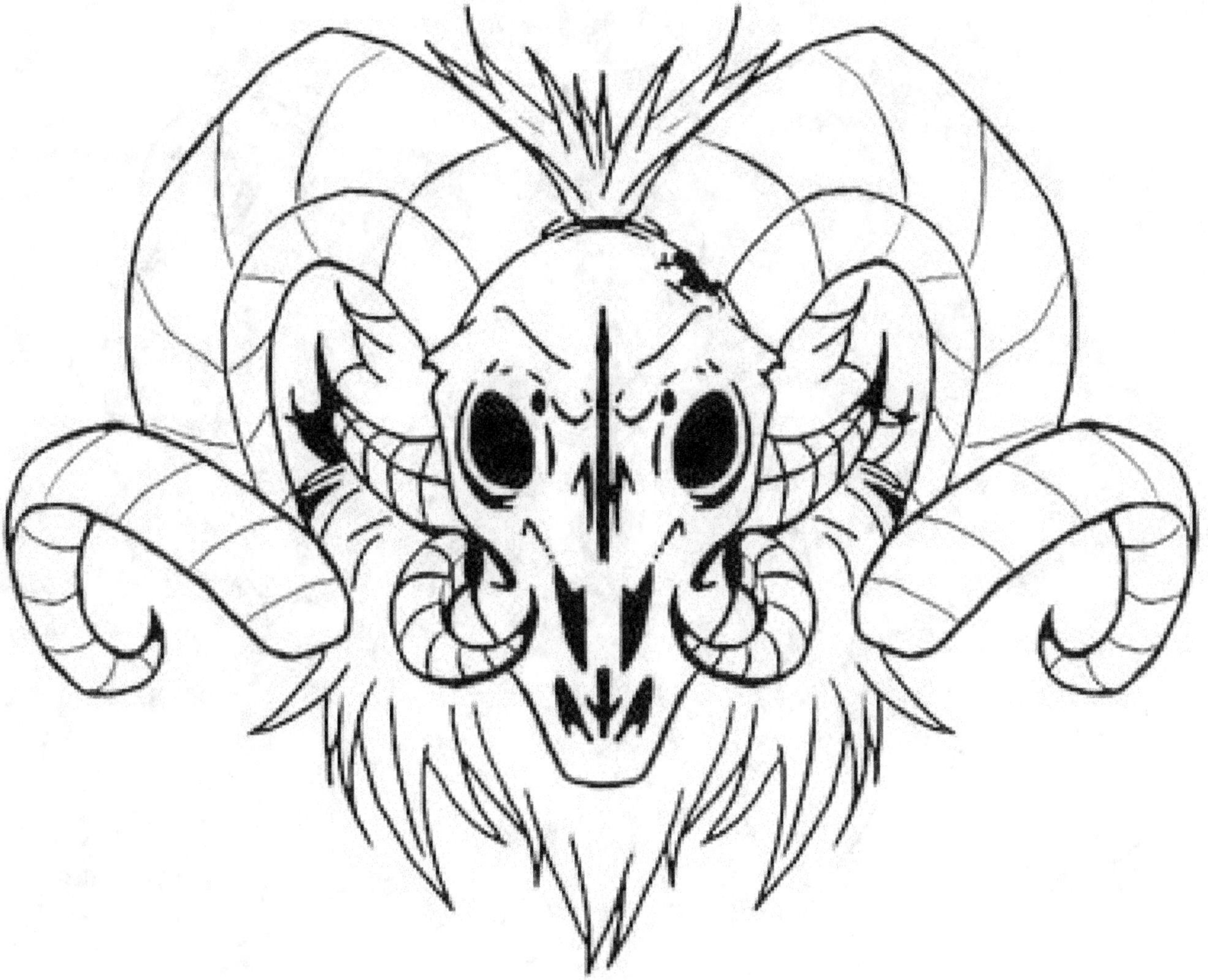

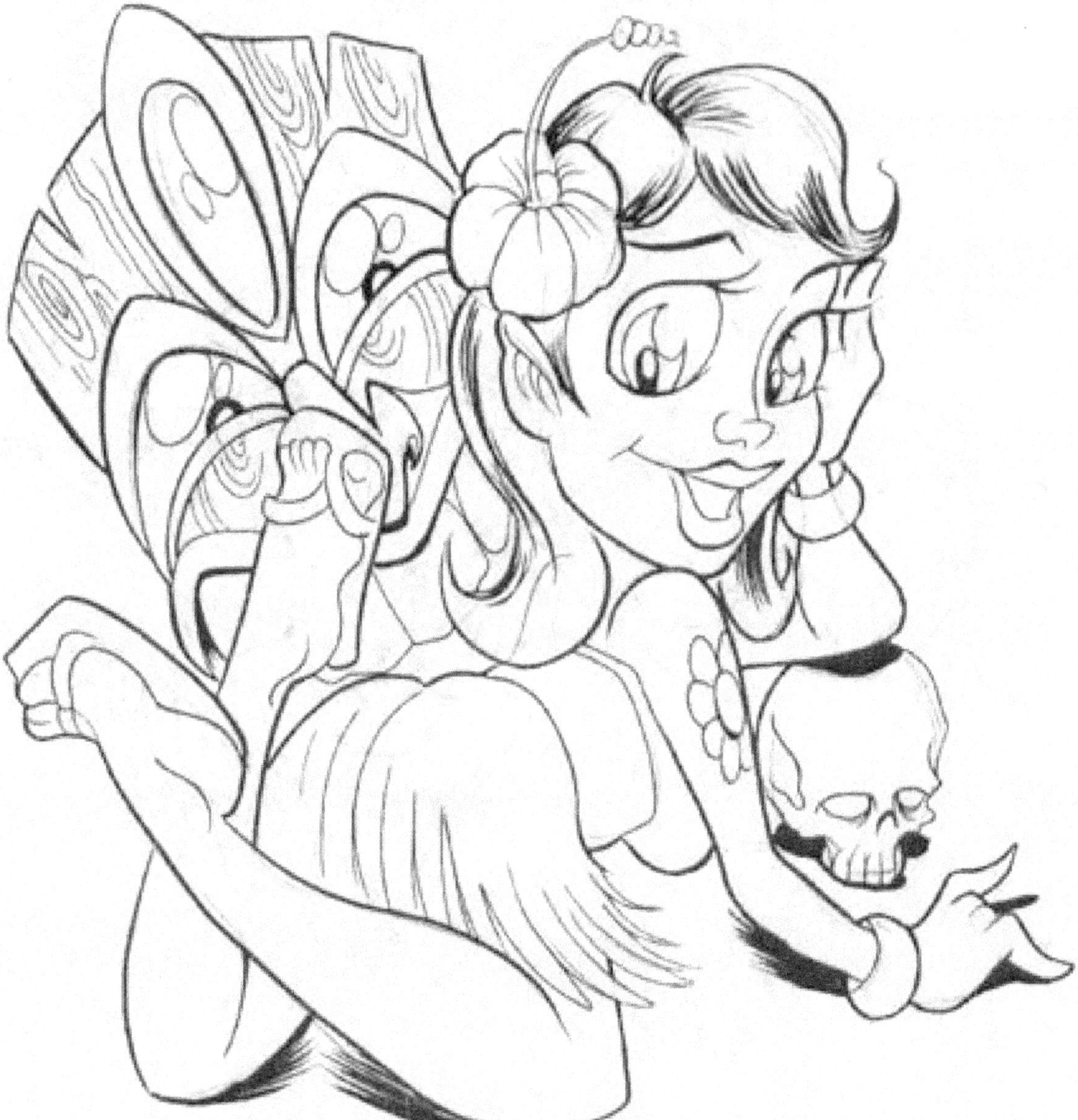

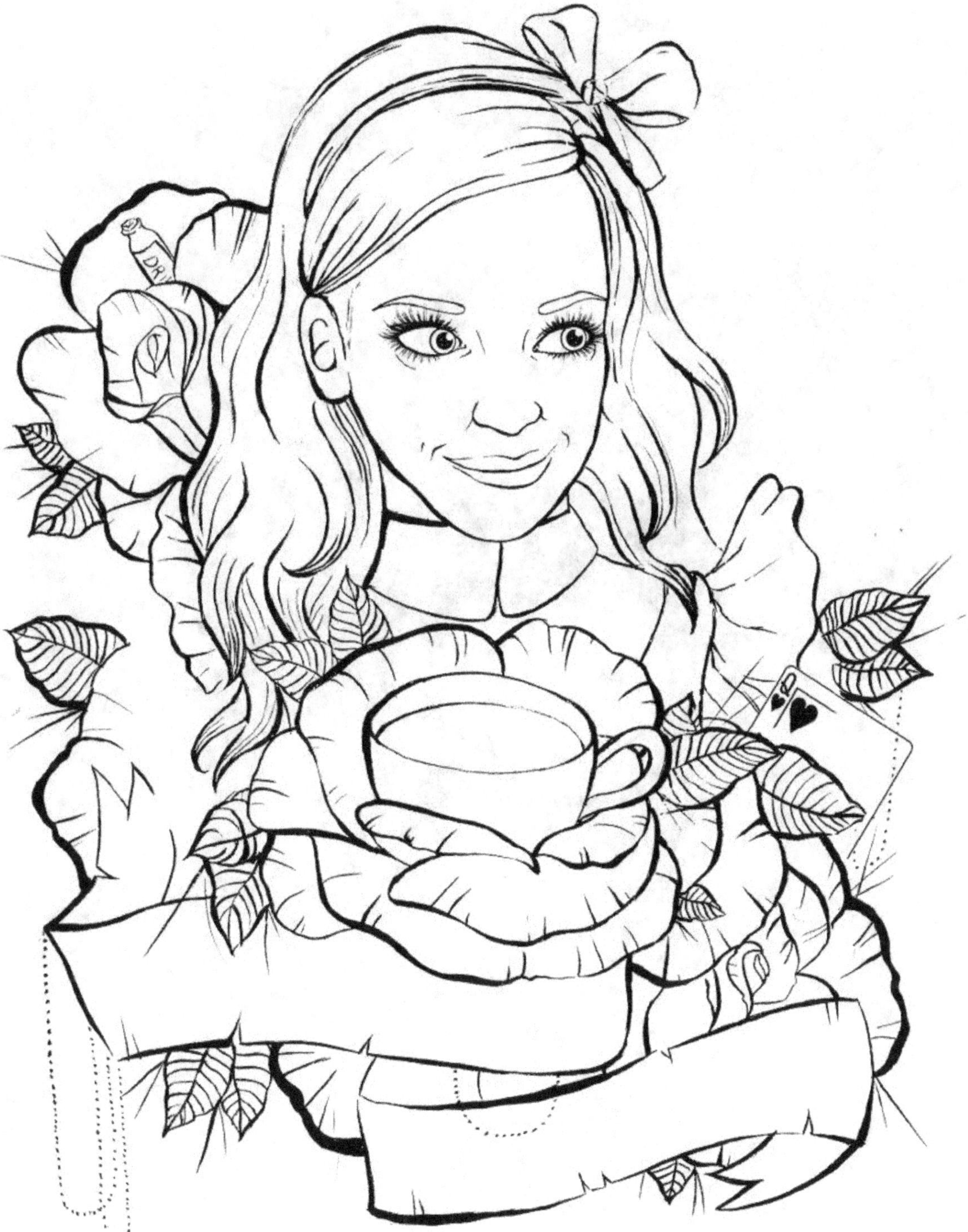

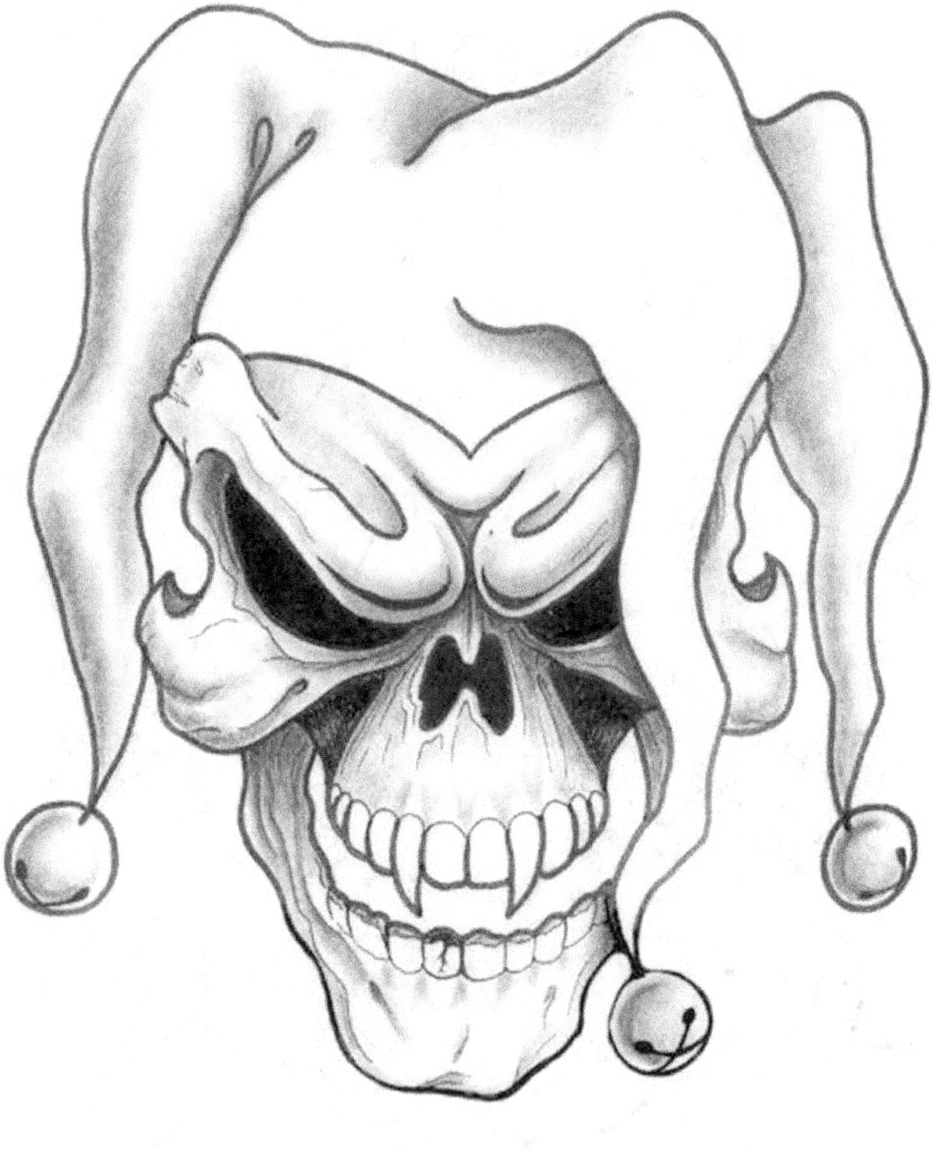

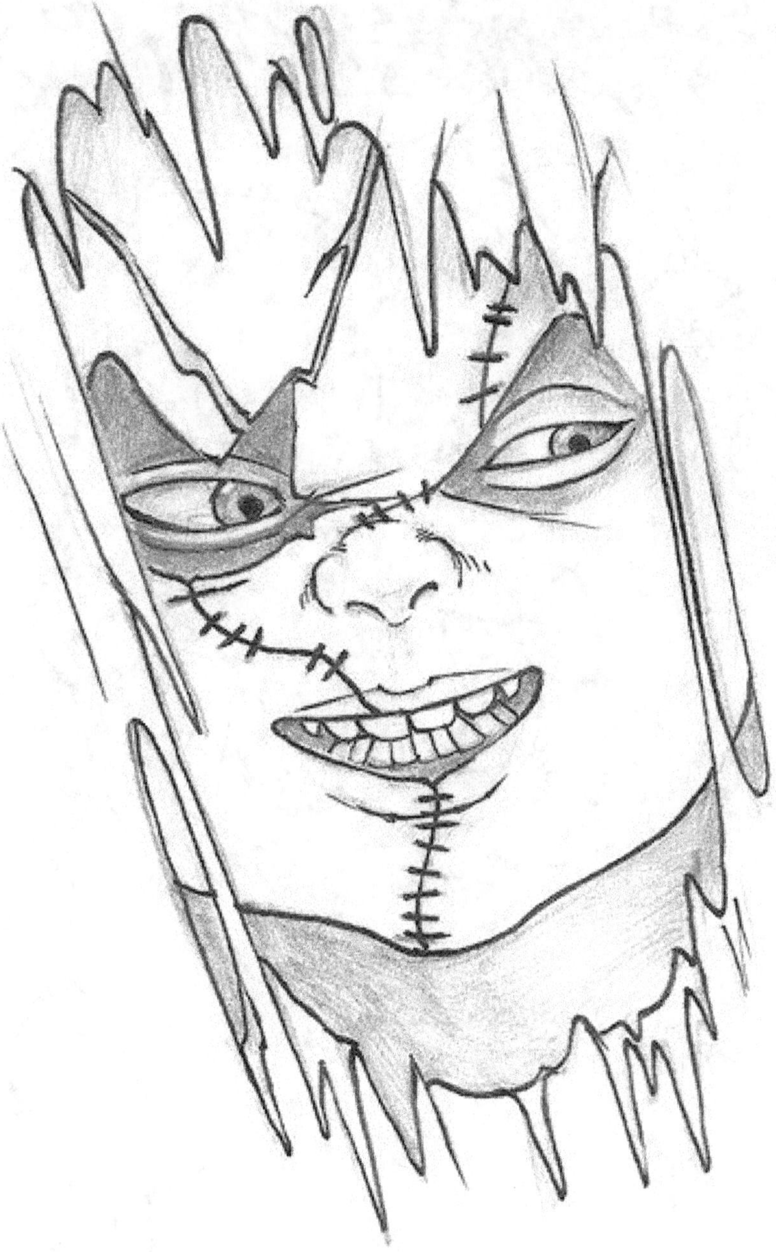

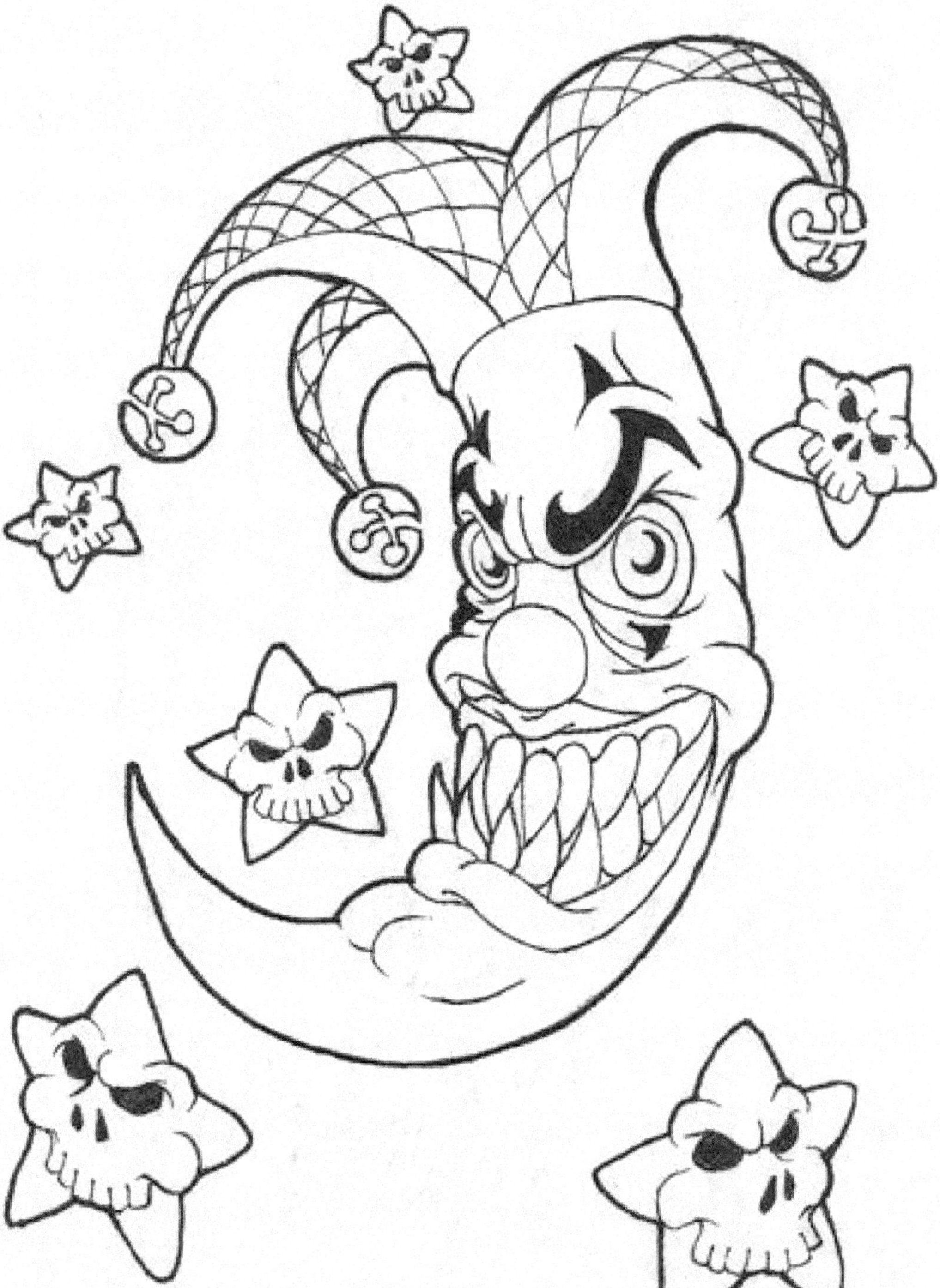

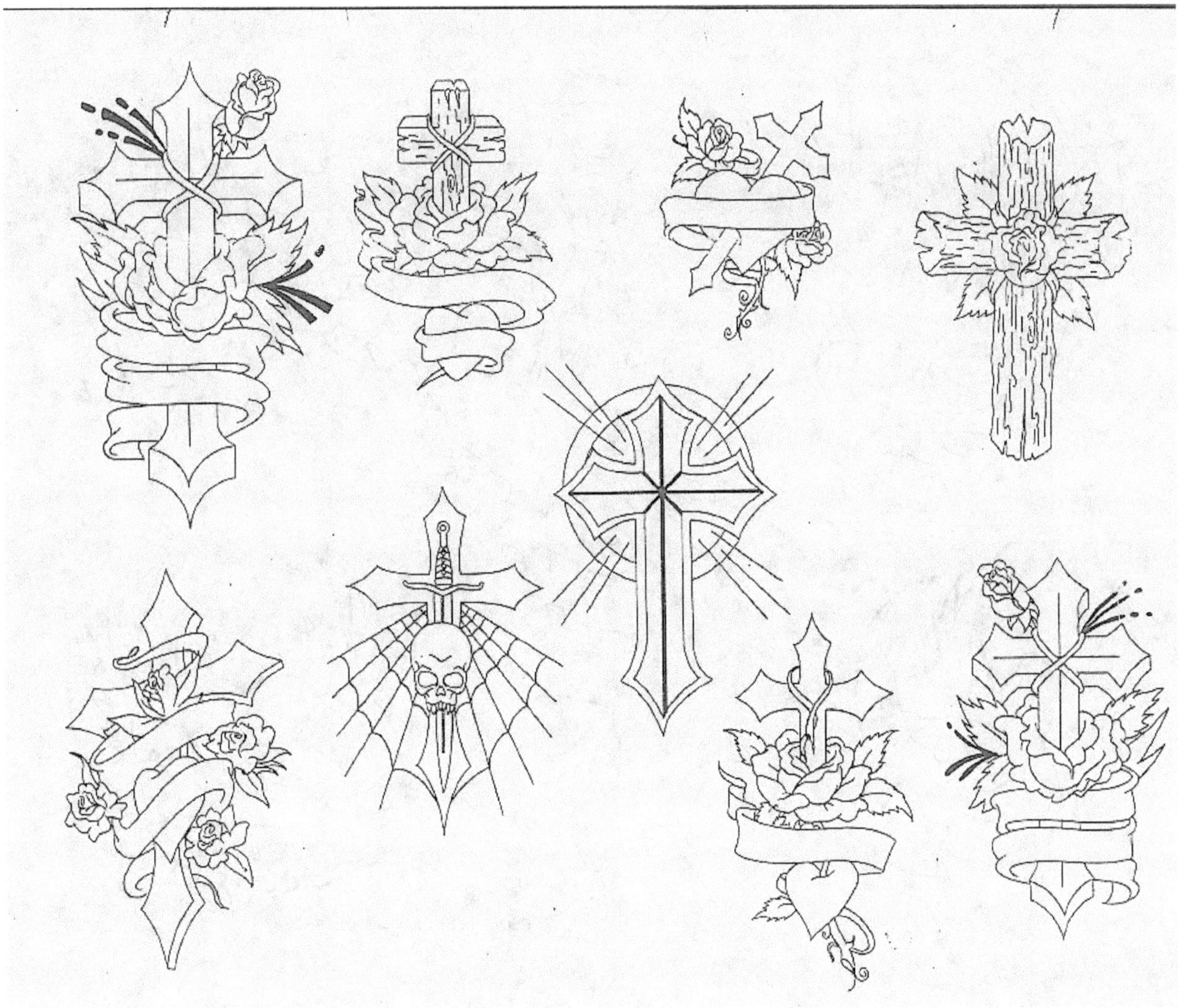

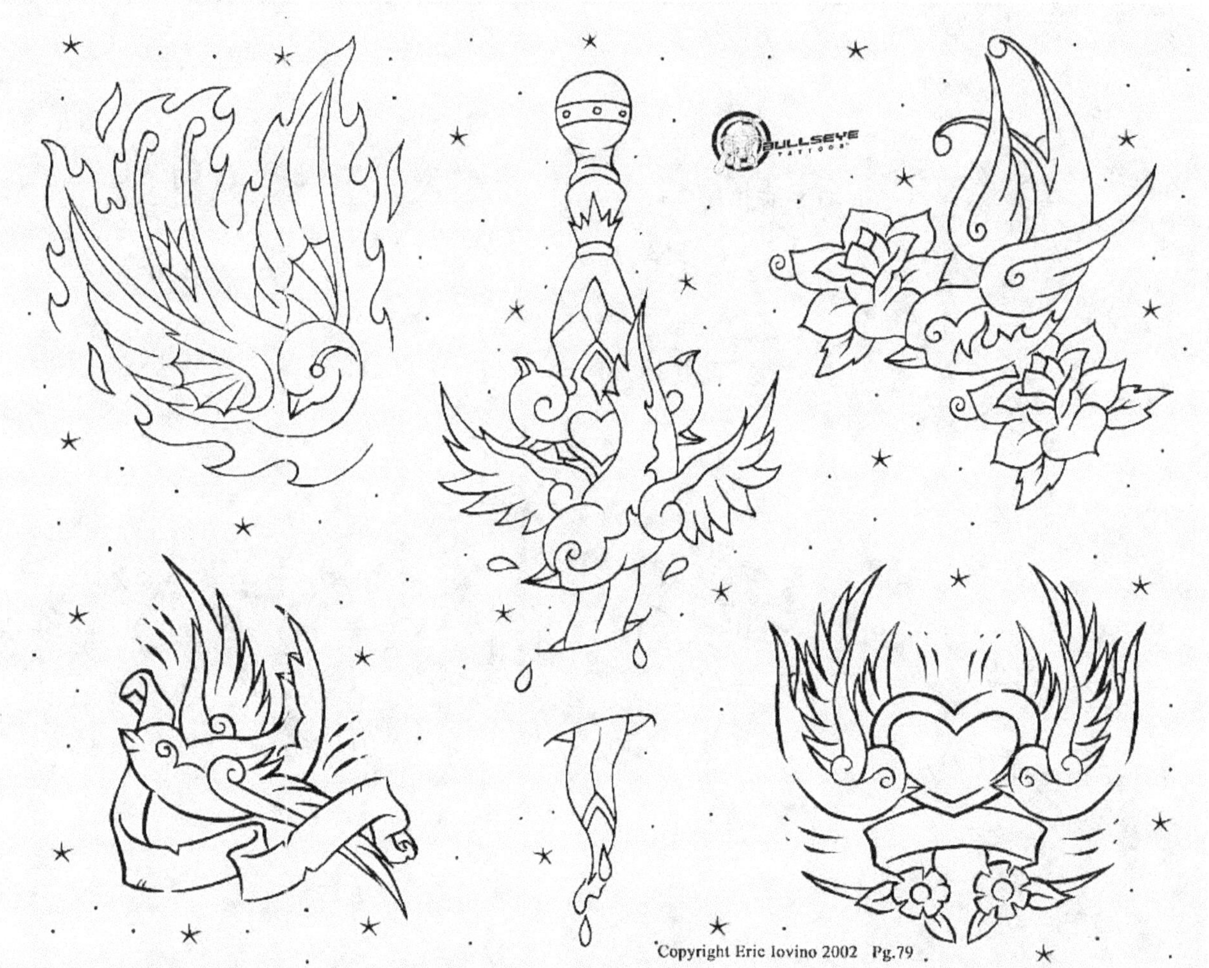

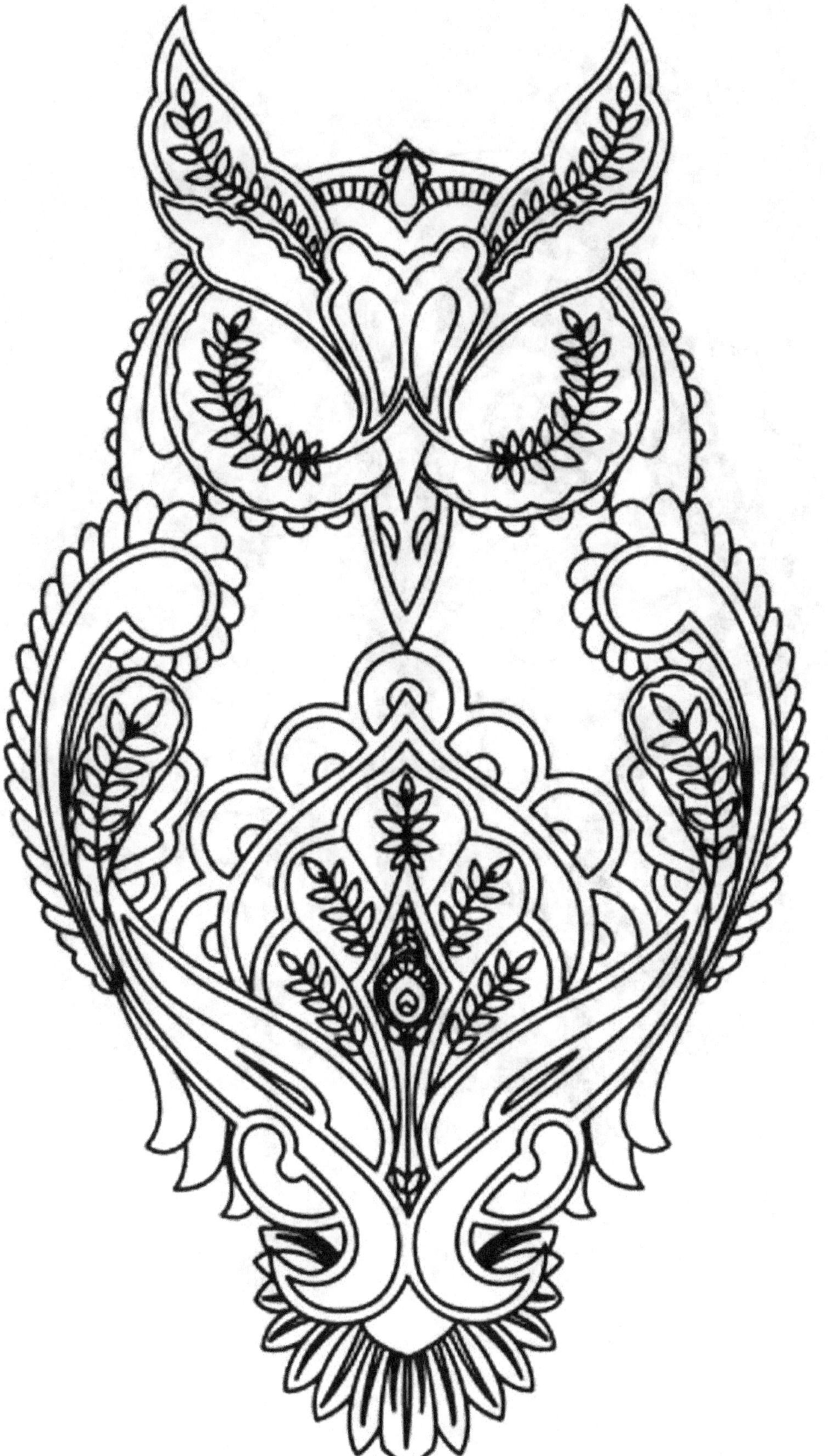

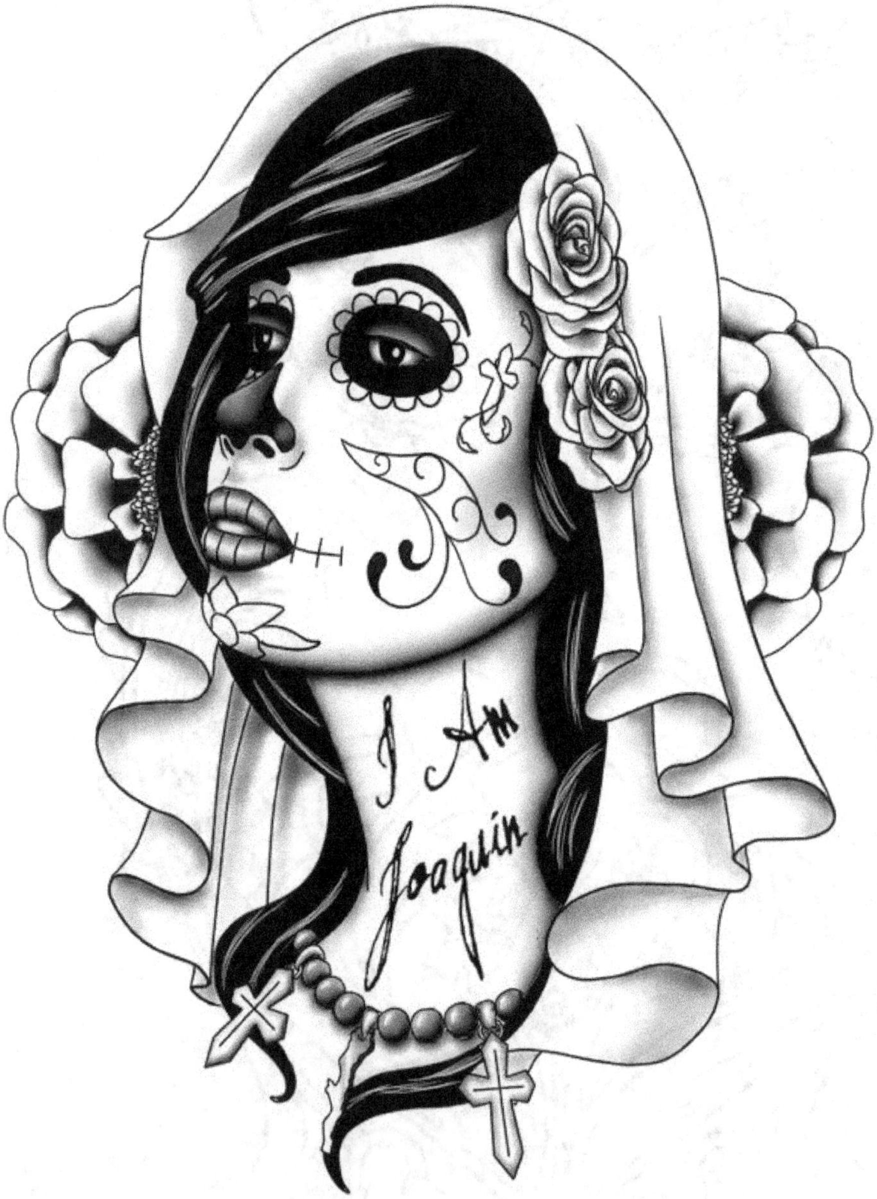
I Am
Joaquin

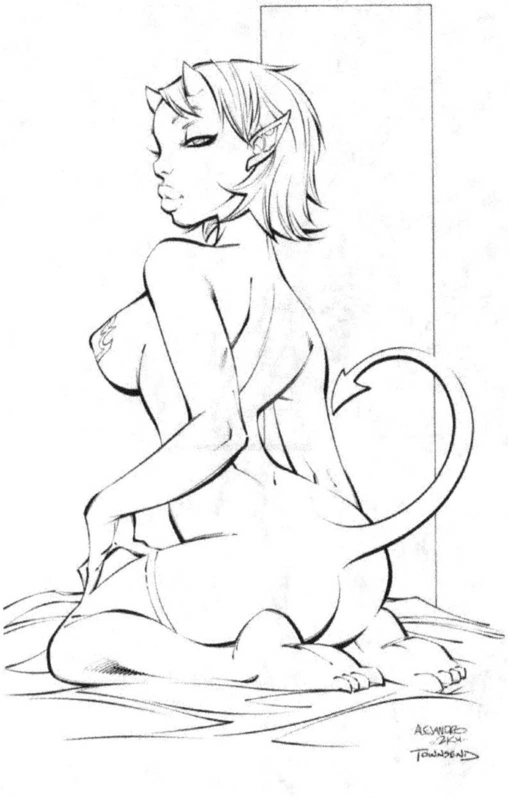
TOWNSEND
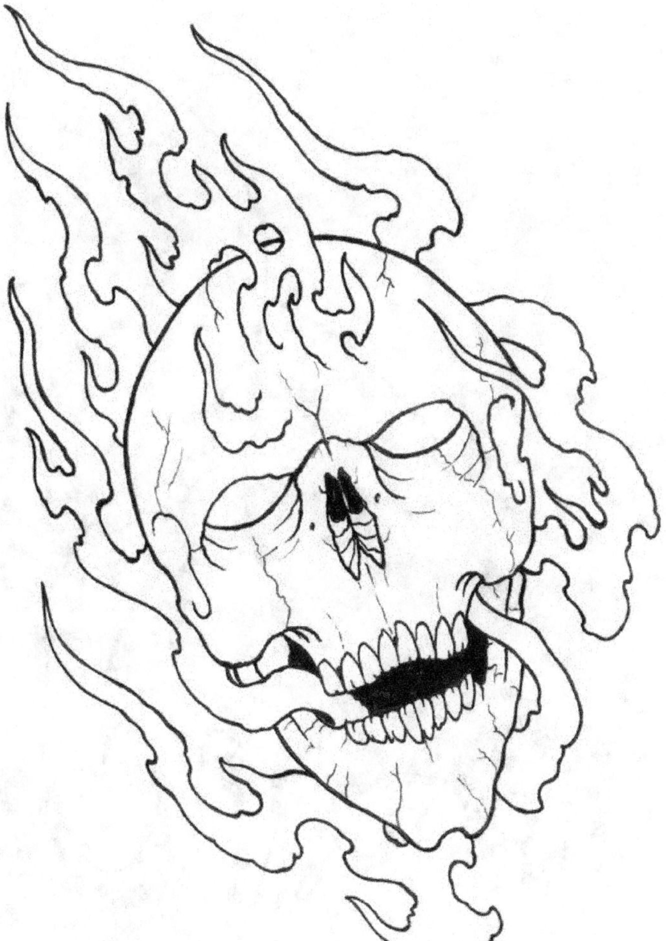

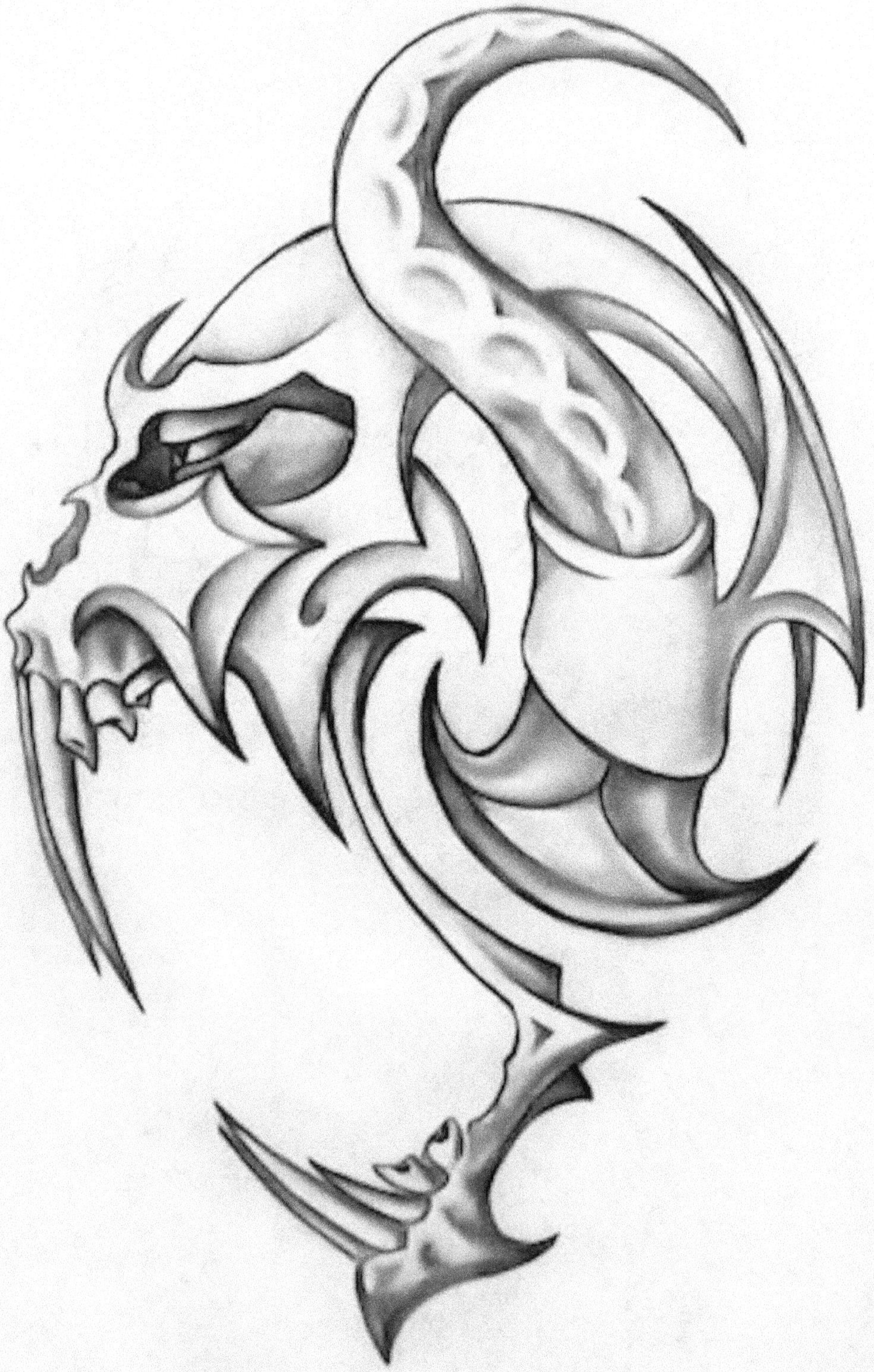

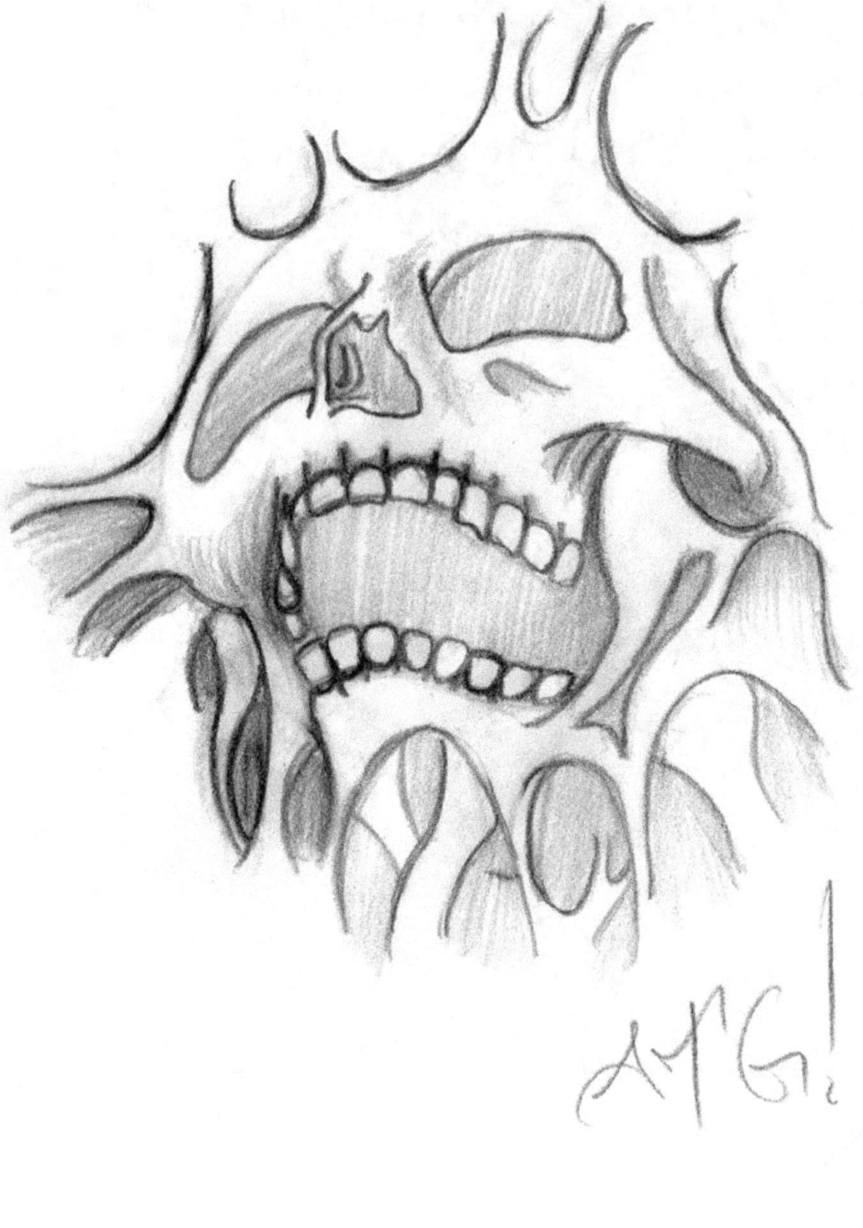

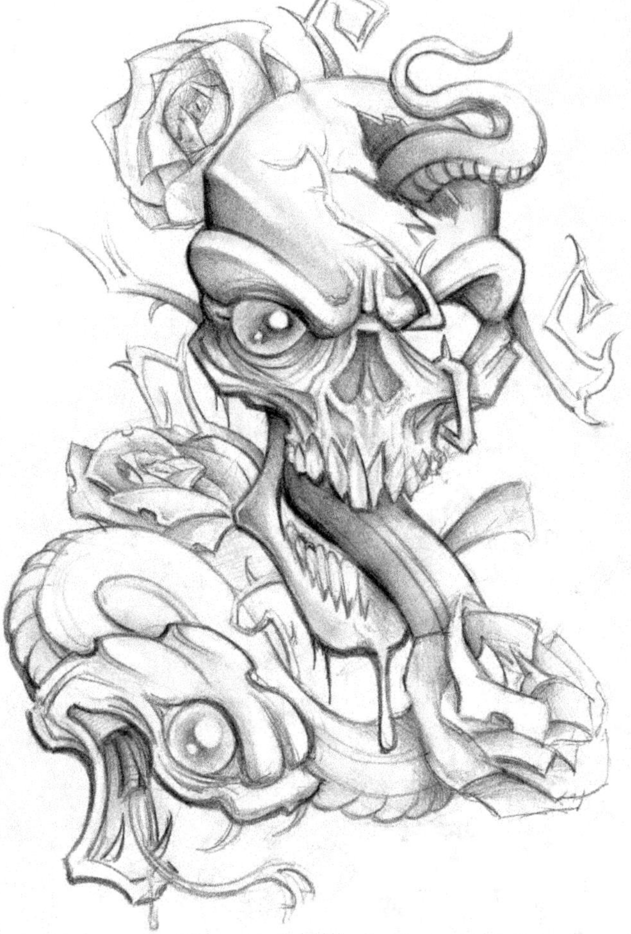

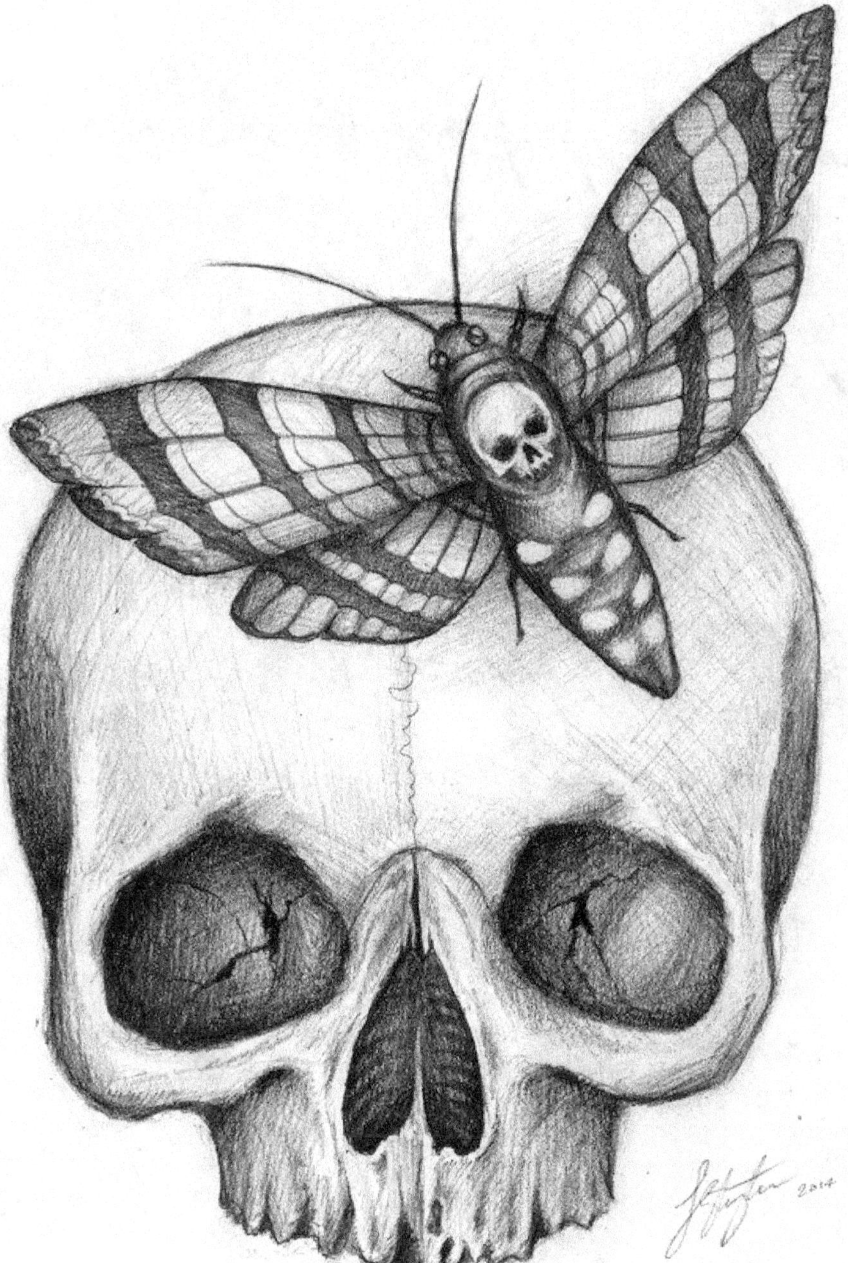

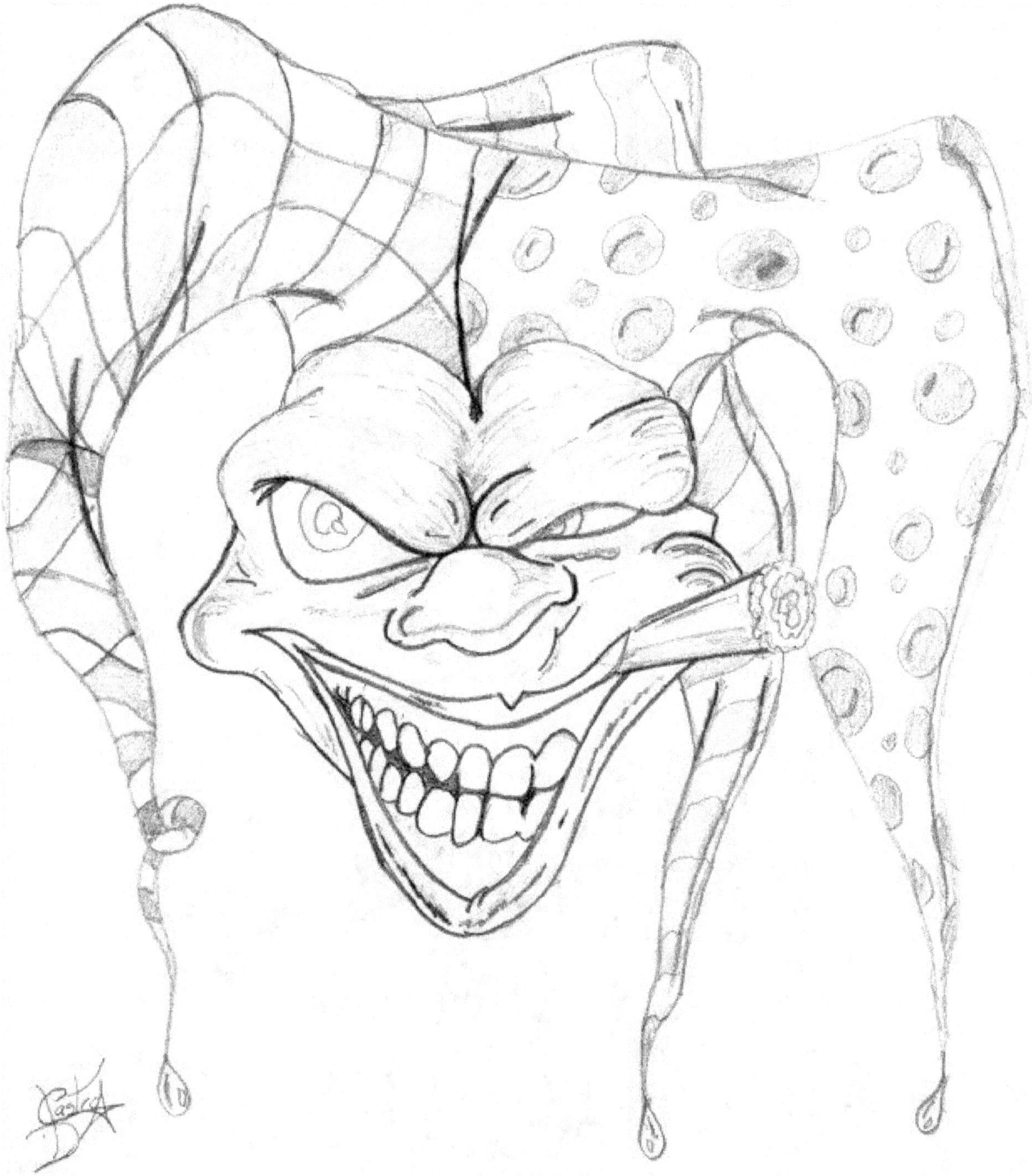

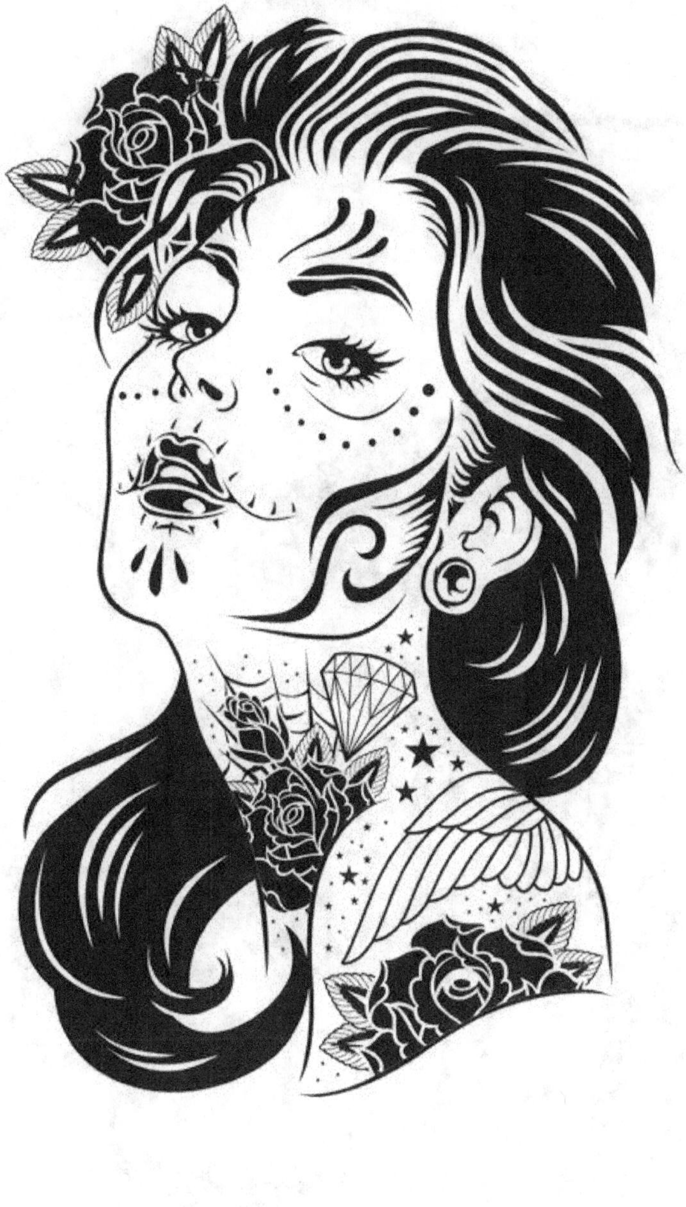

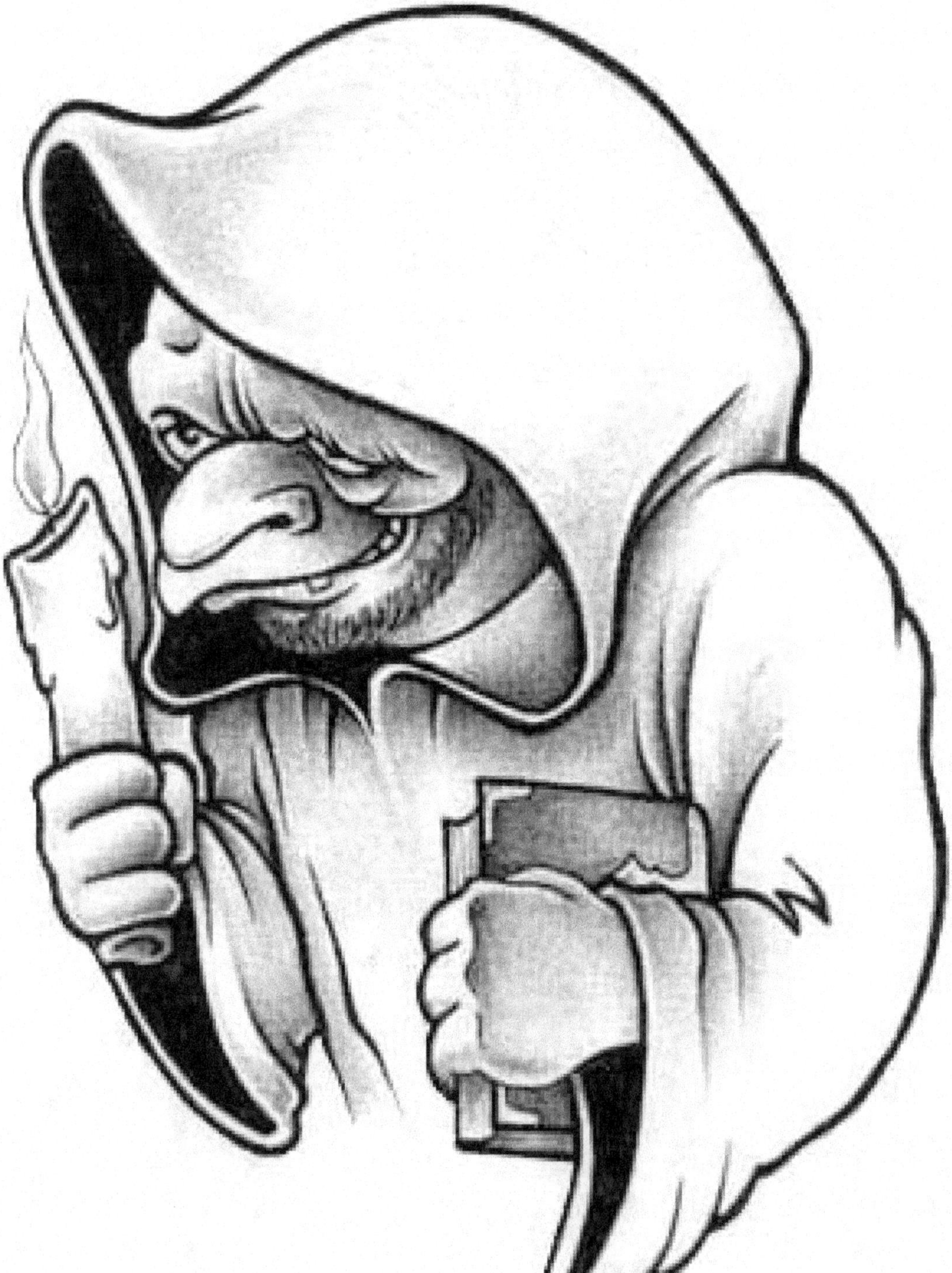

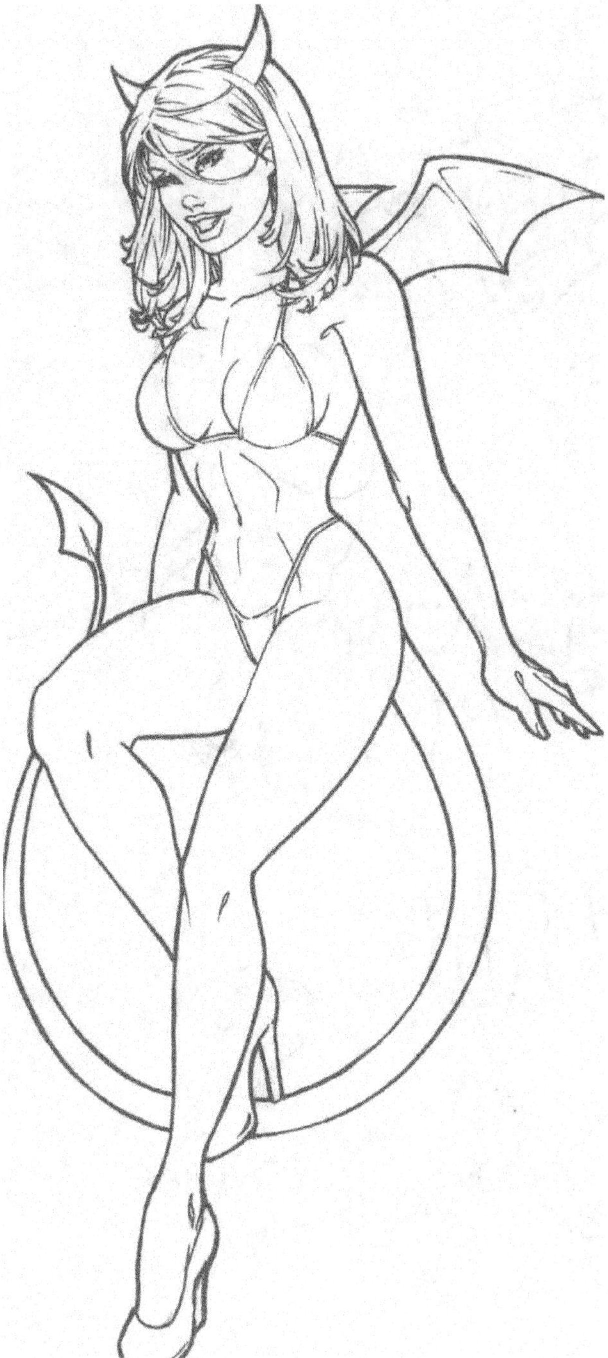

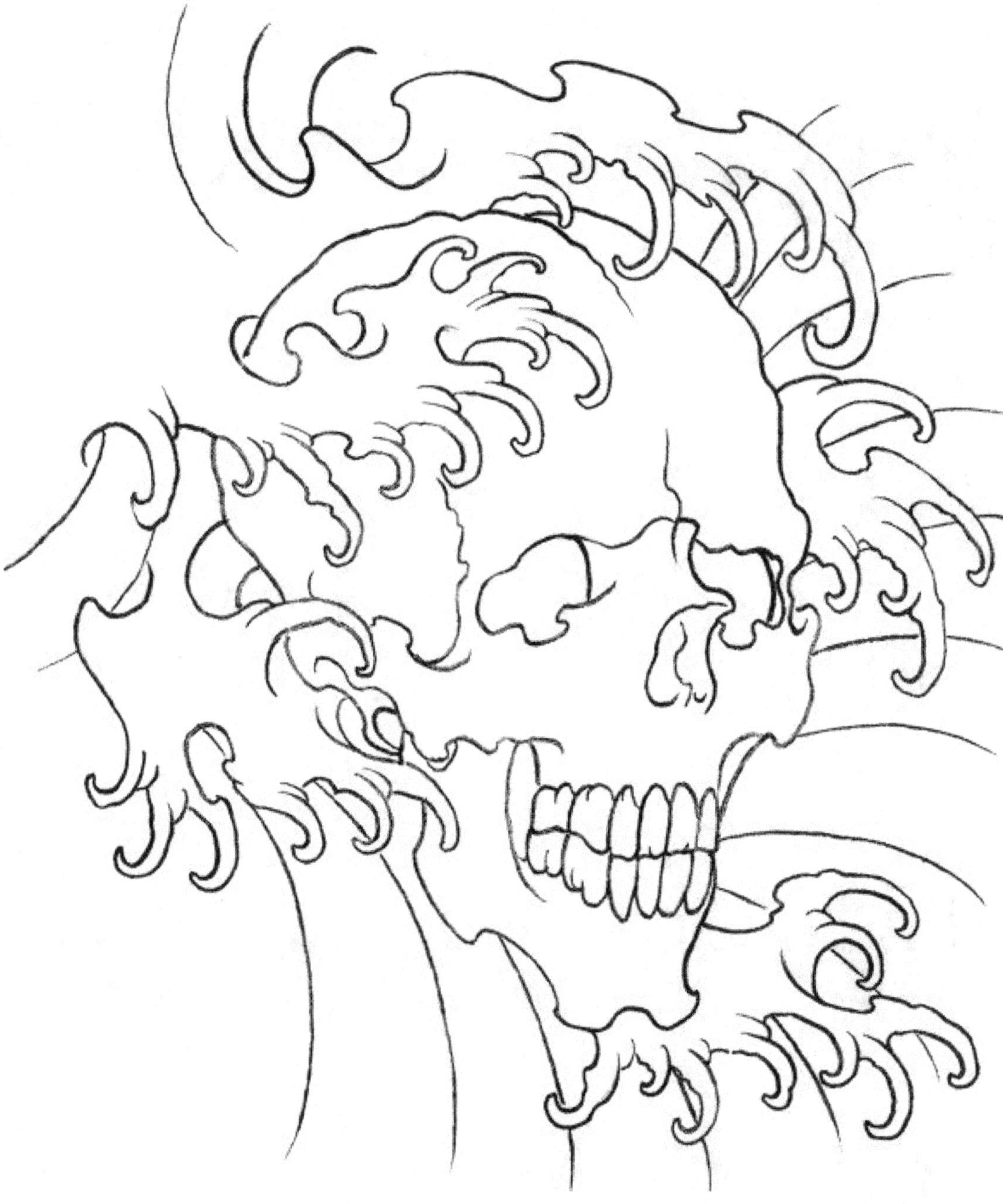

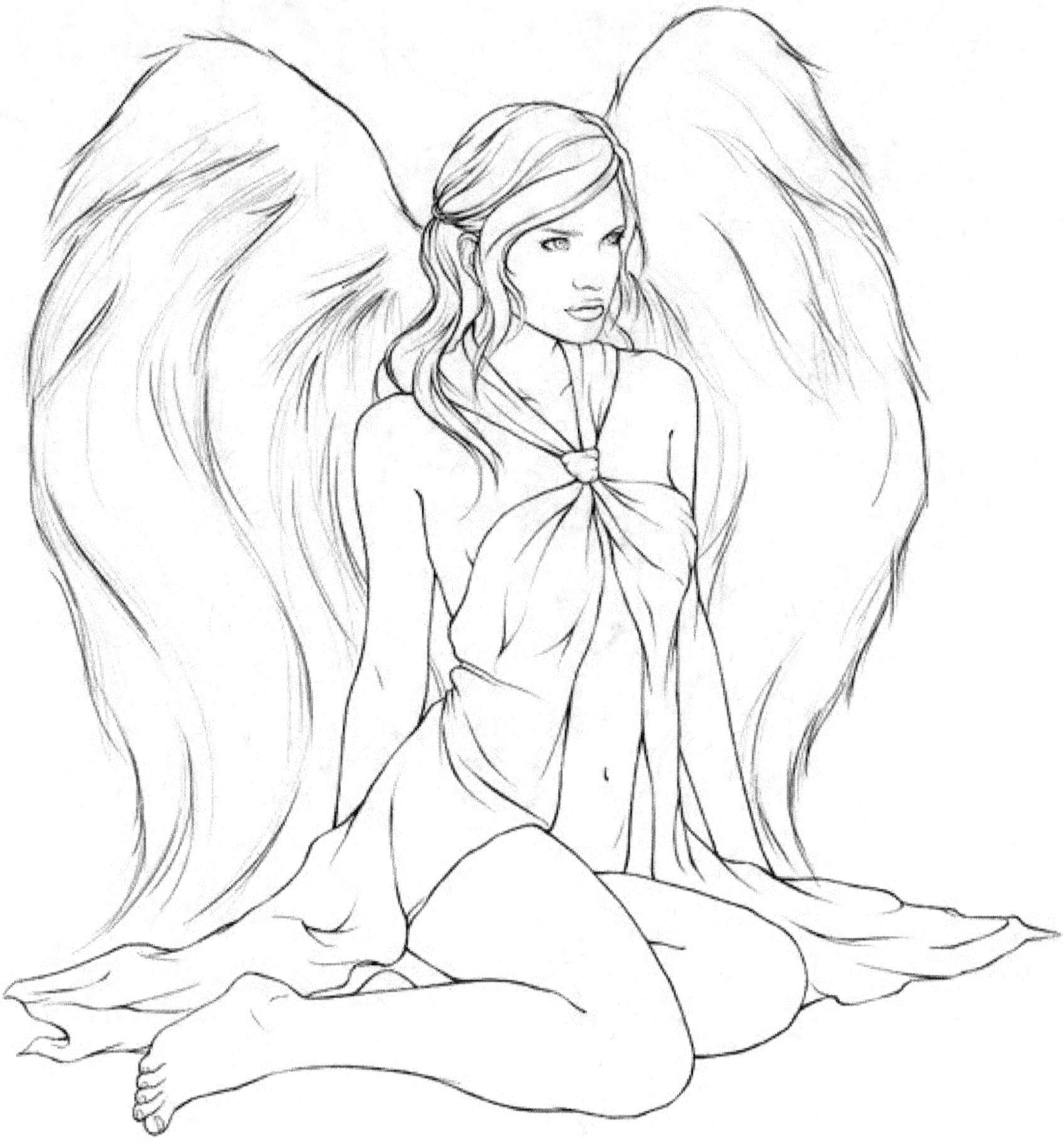

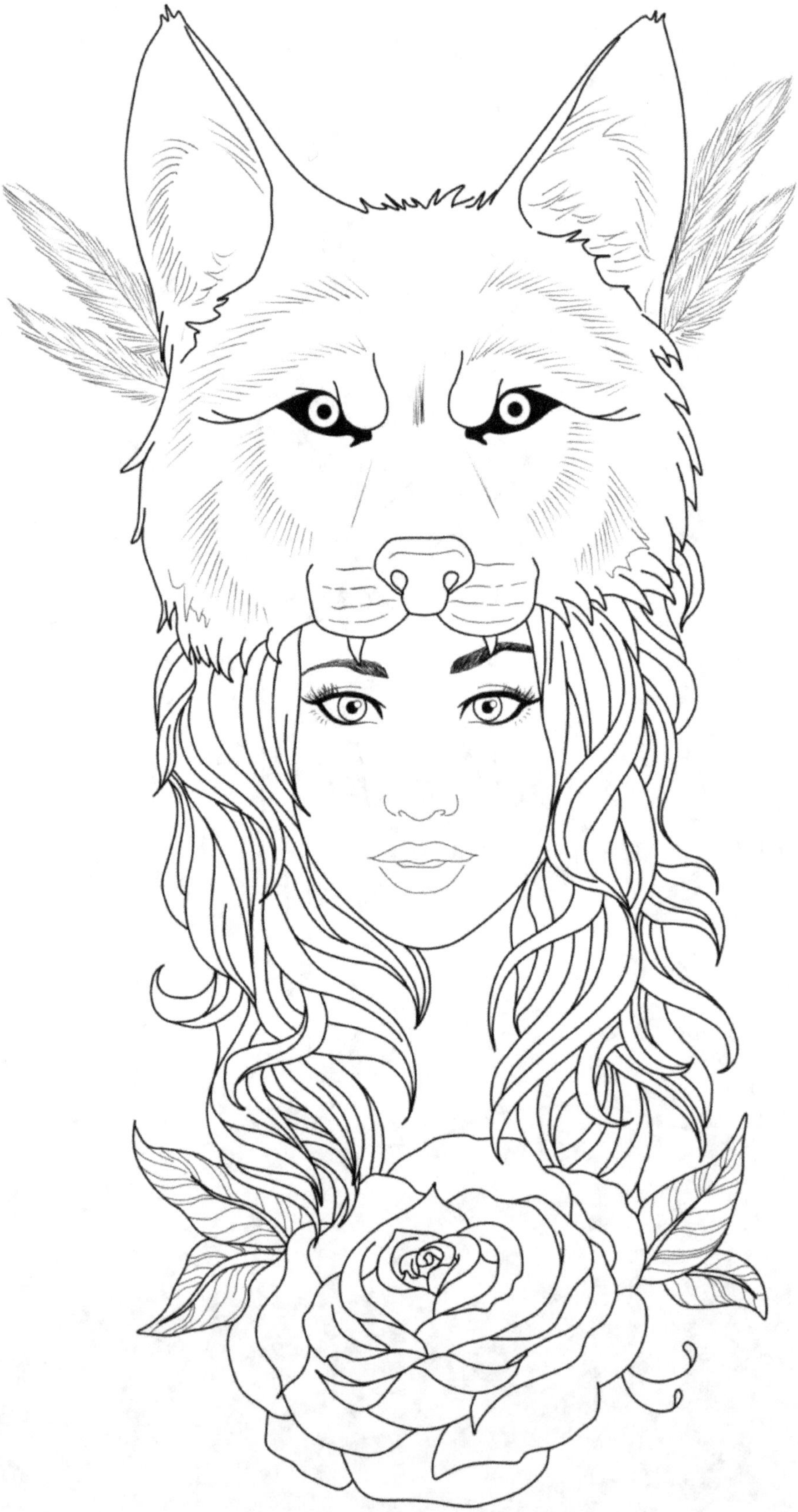

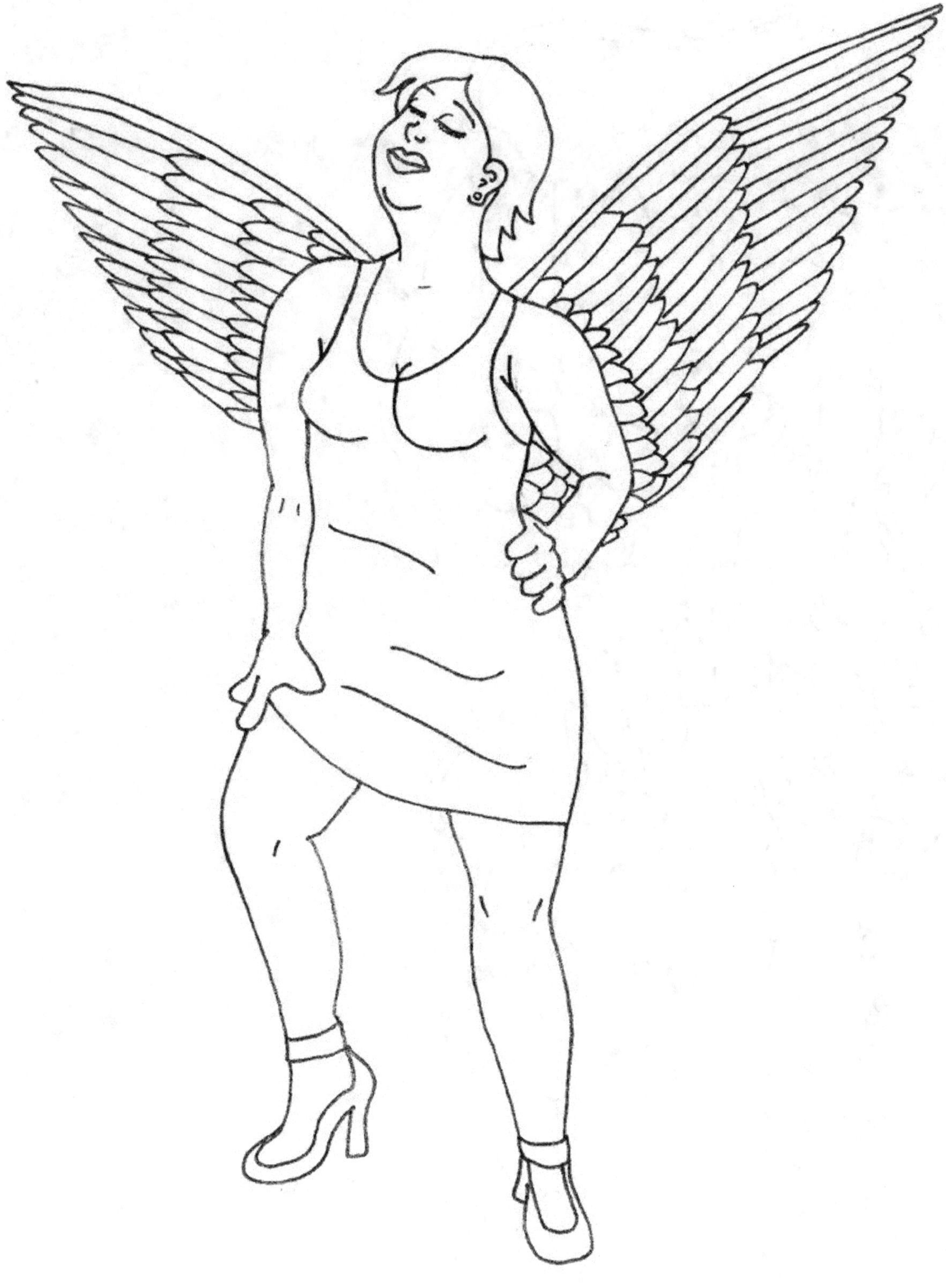

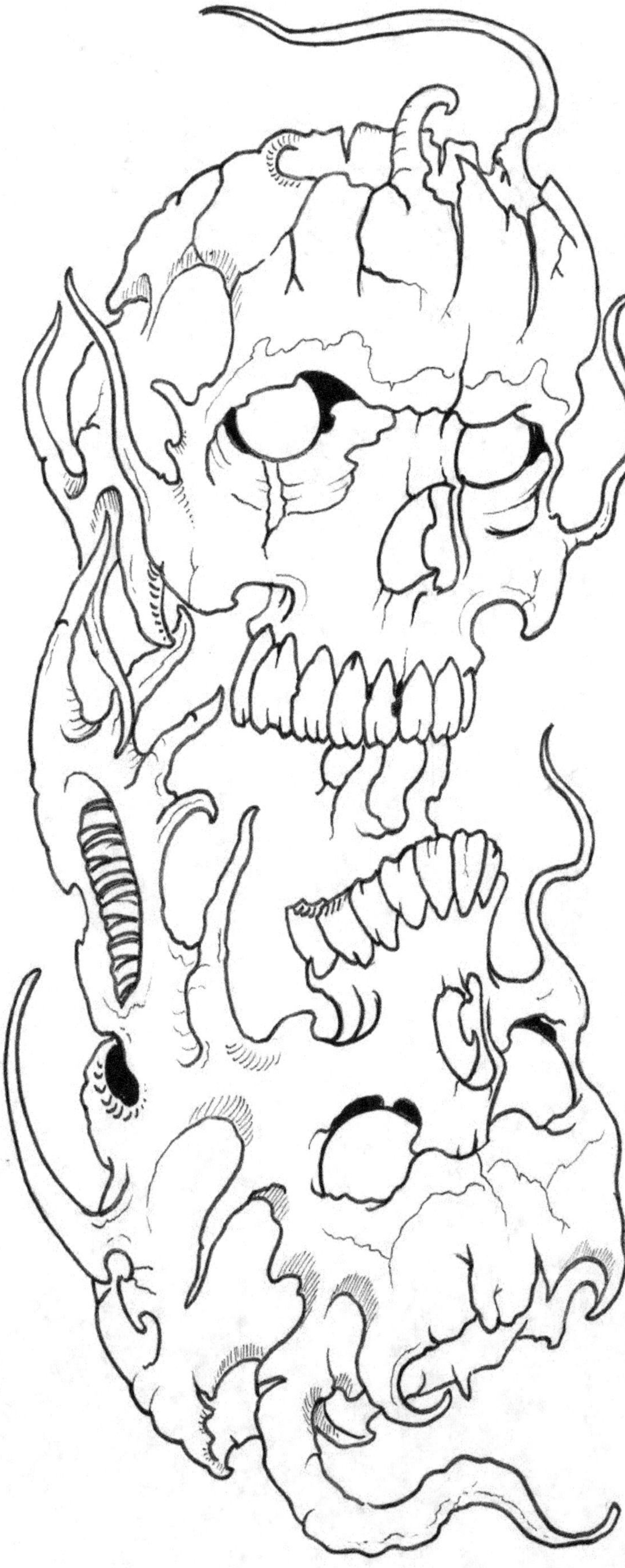

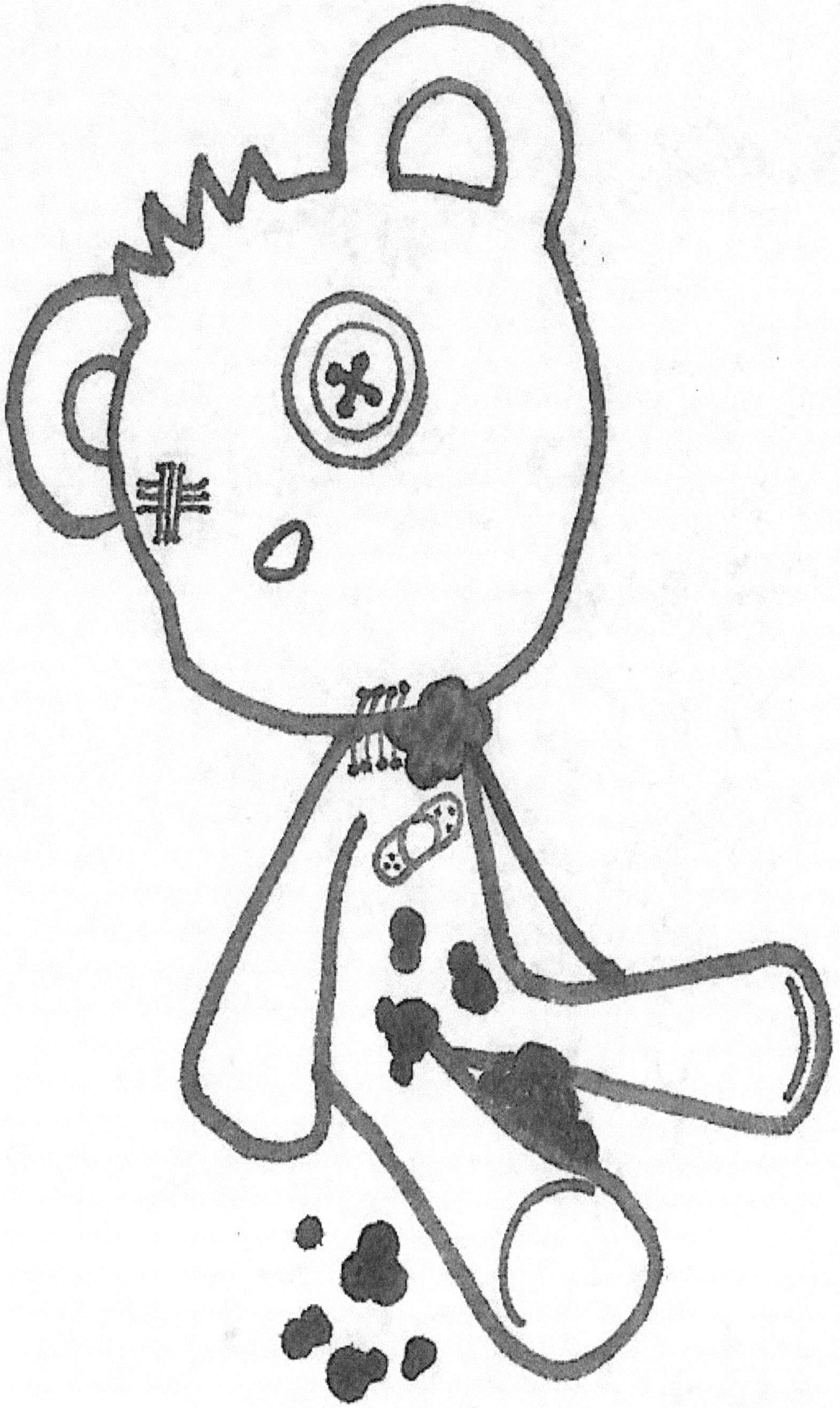

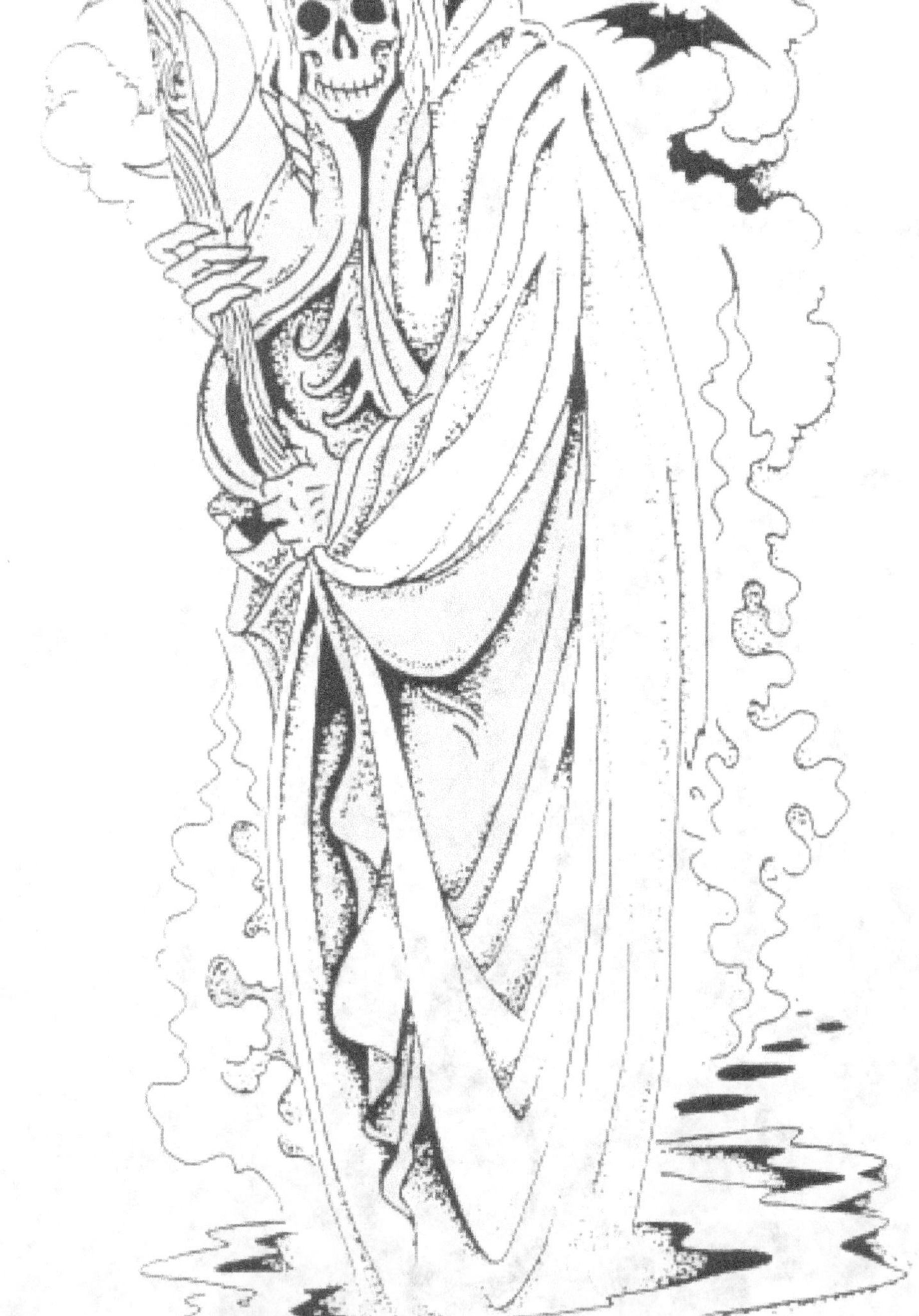

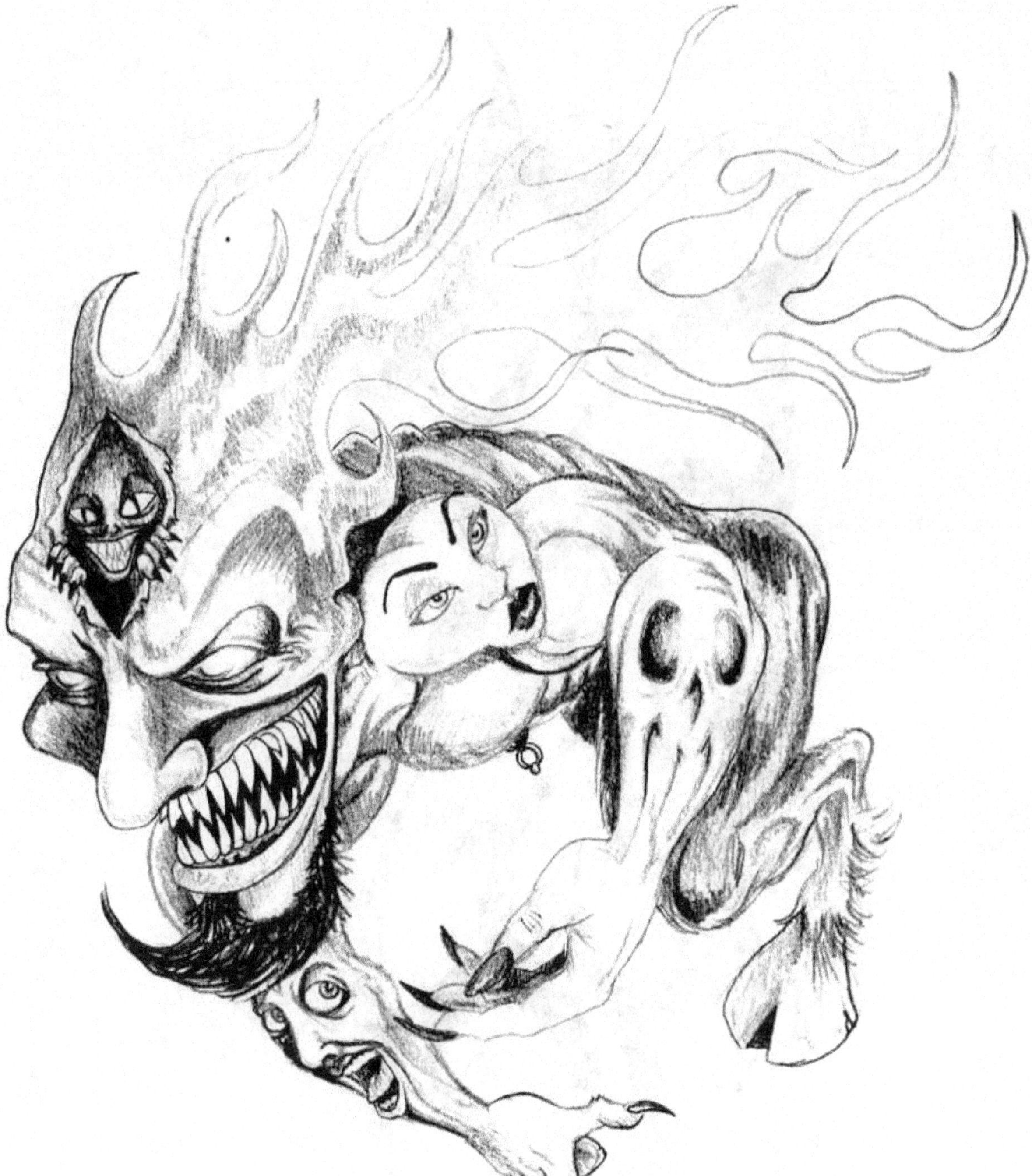

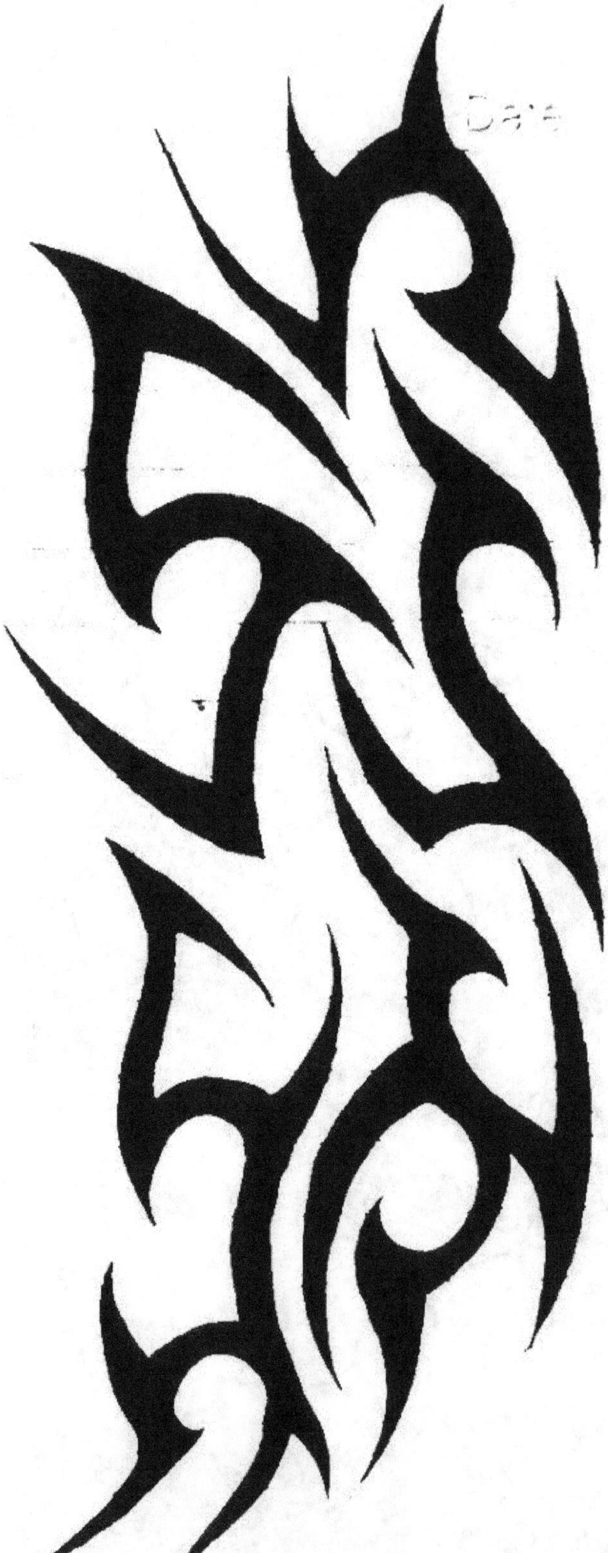

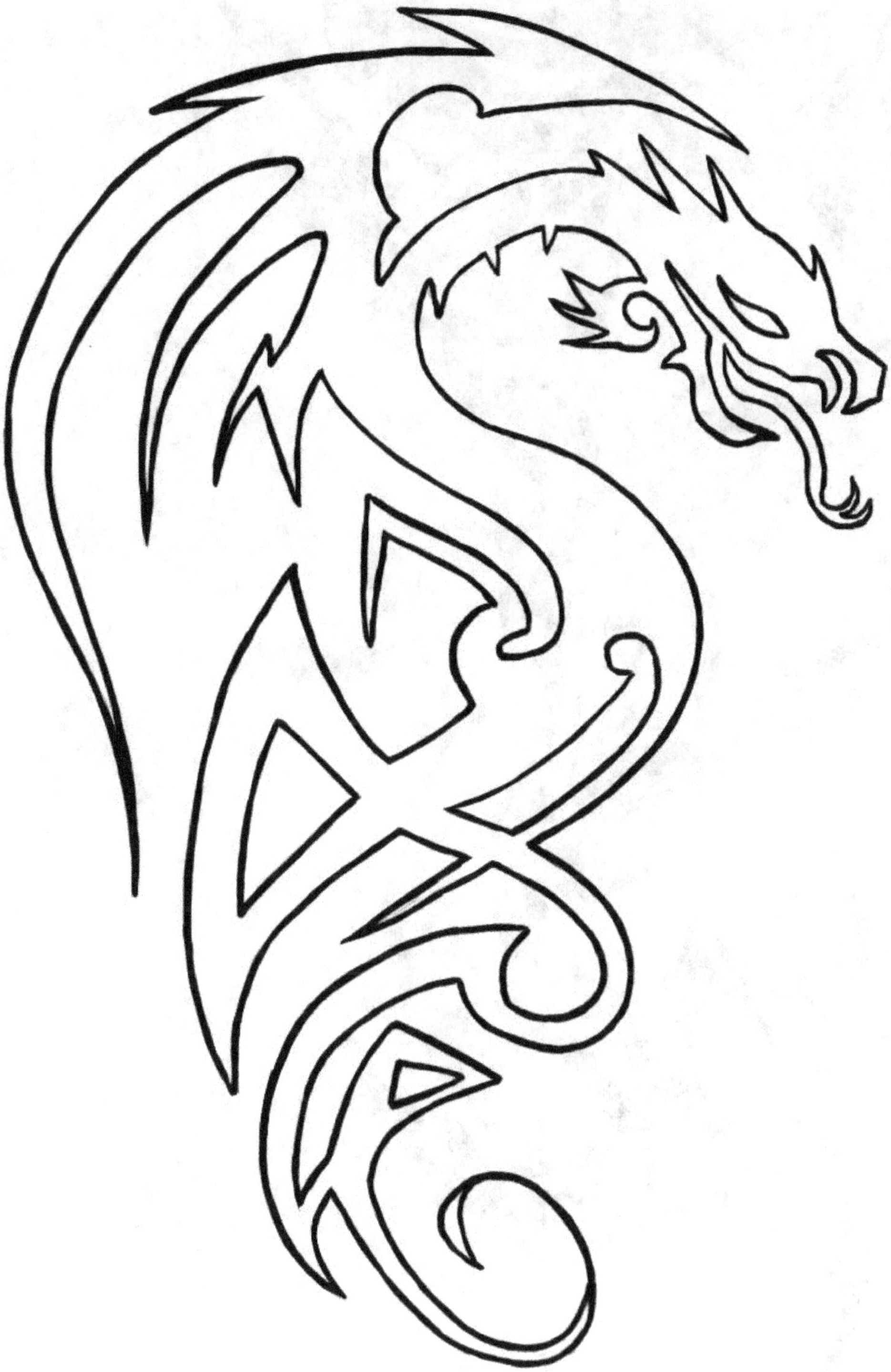

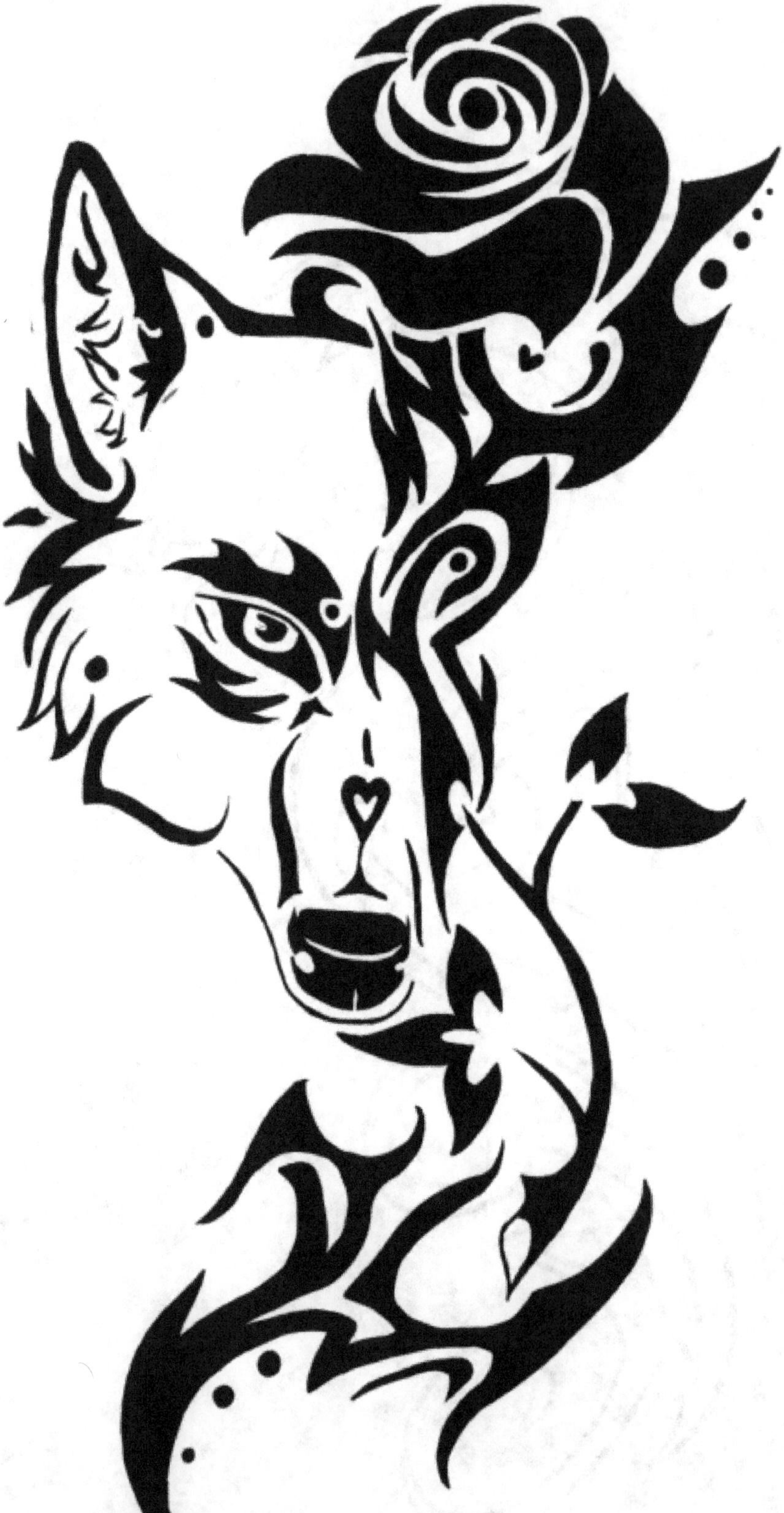

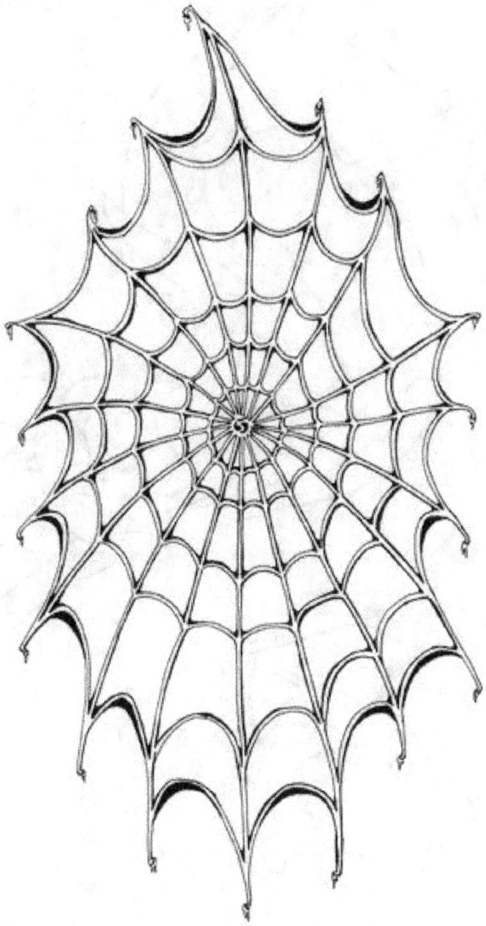

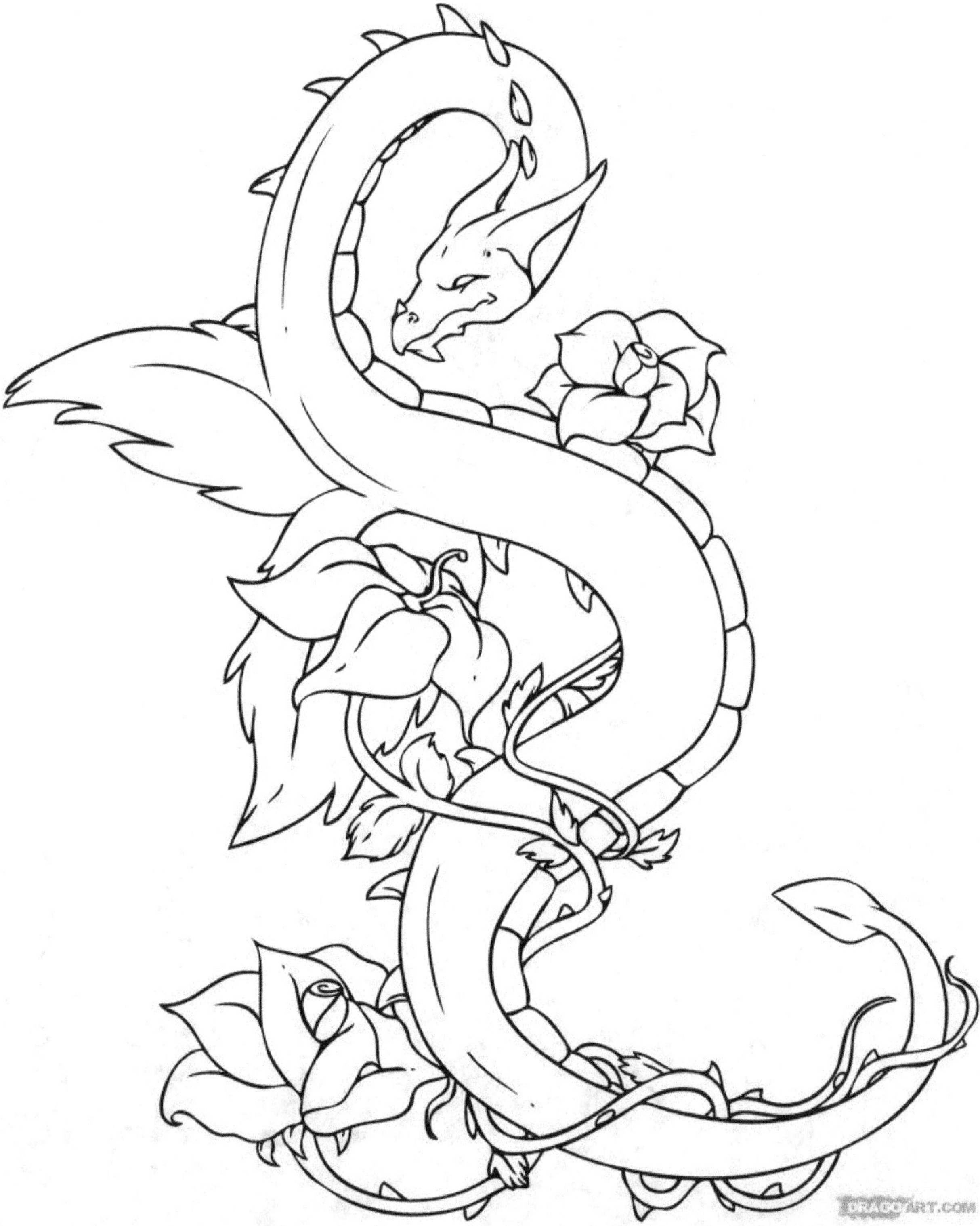
DRAGOART.COM

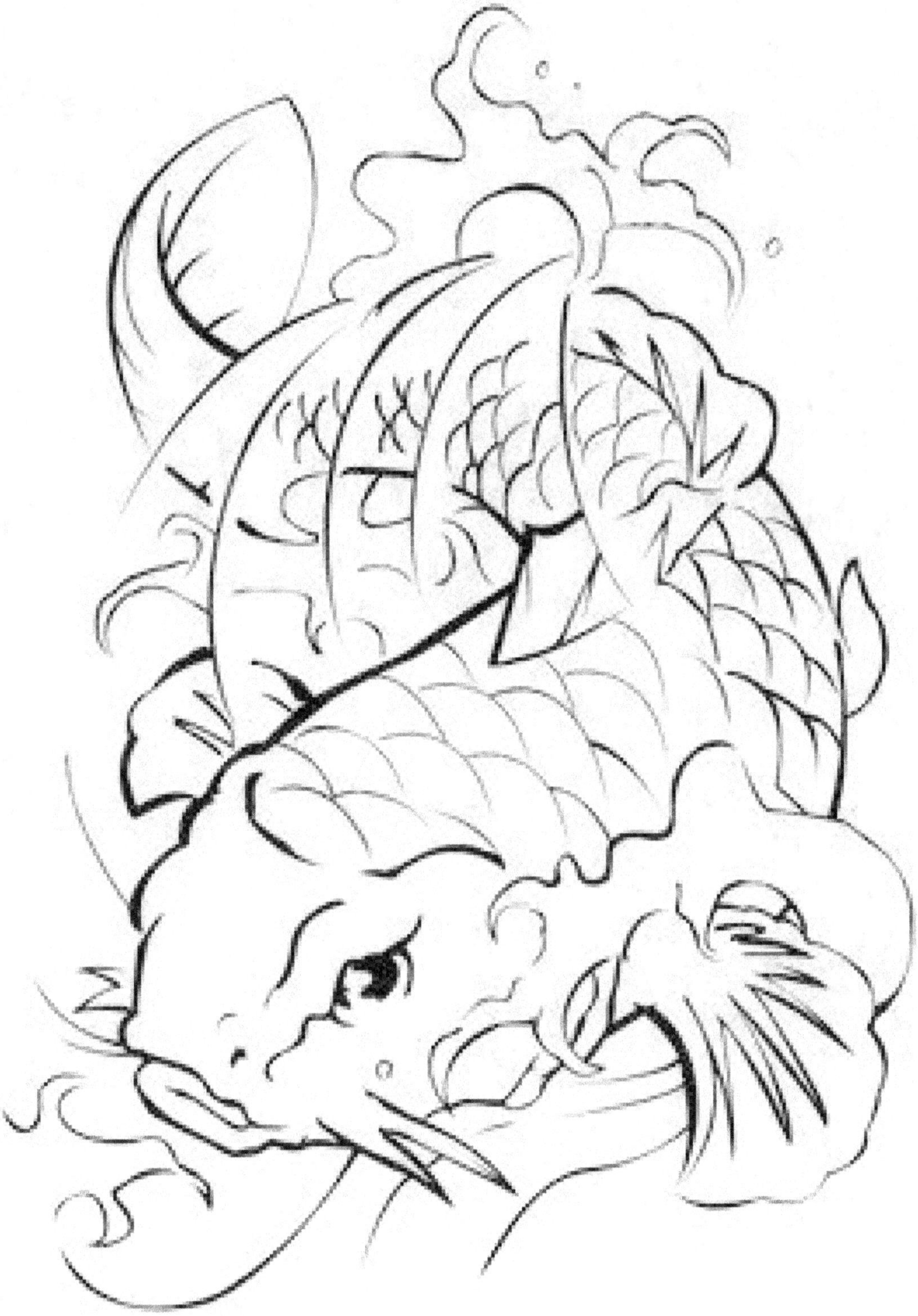

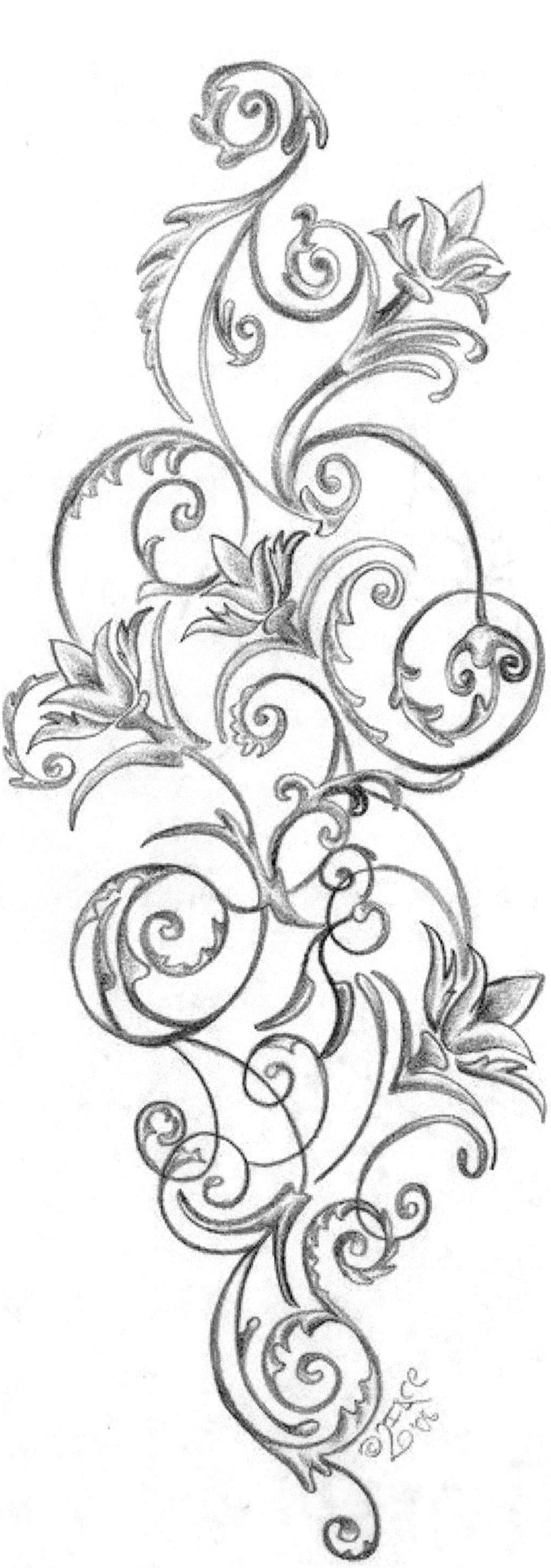

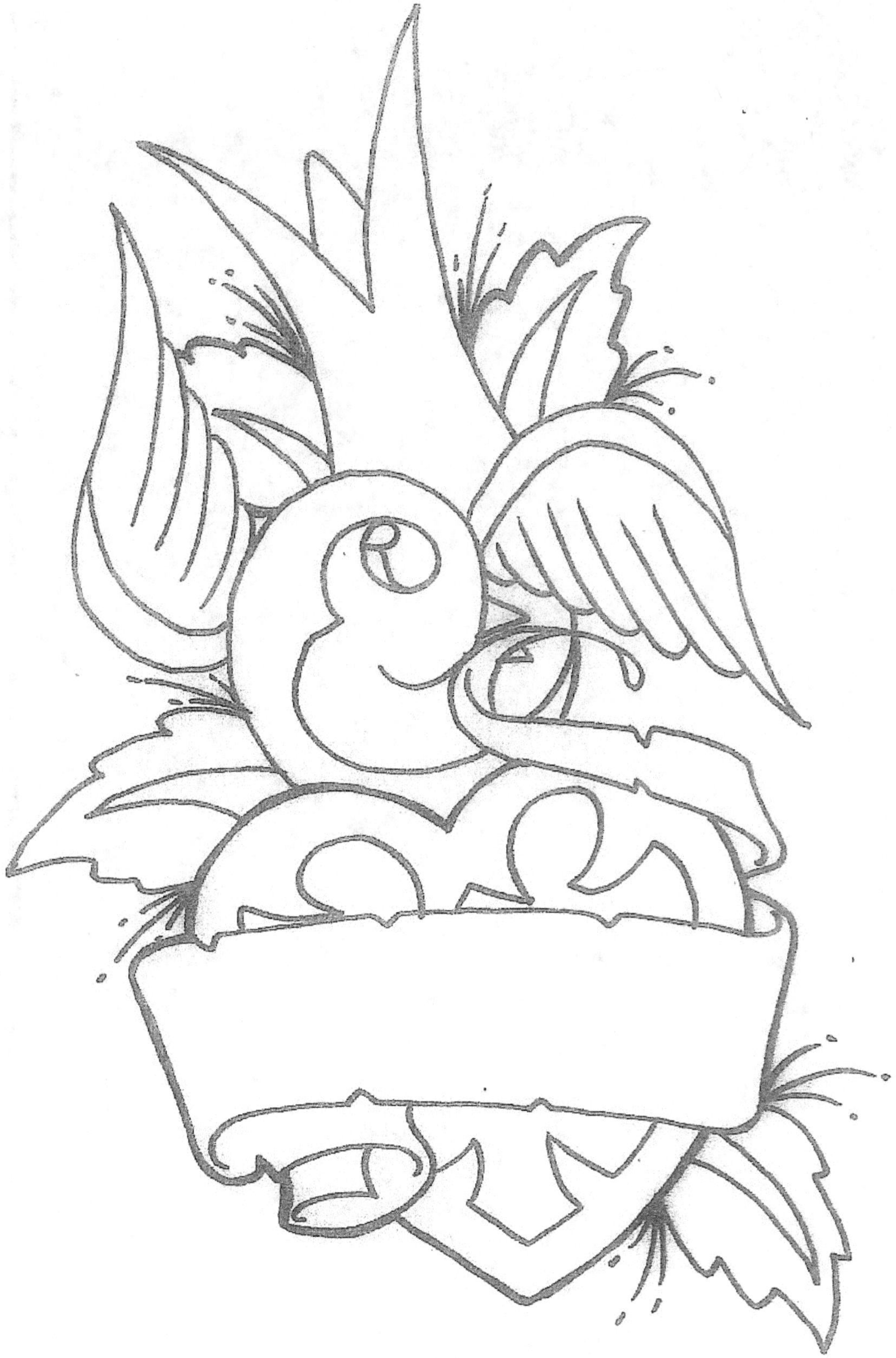

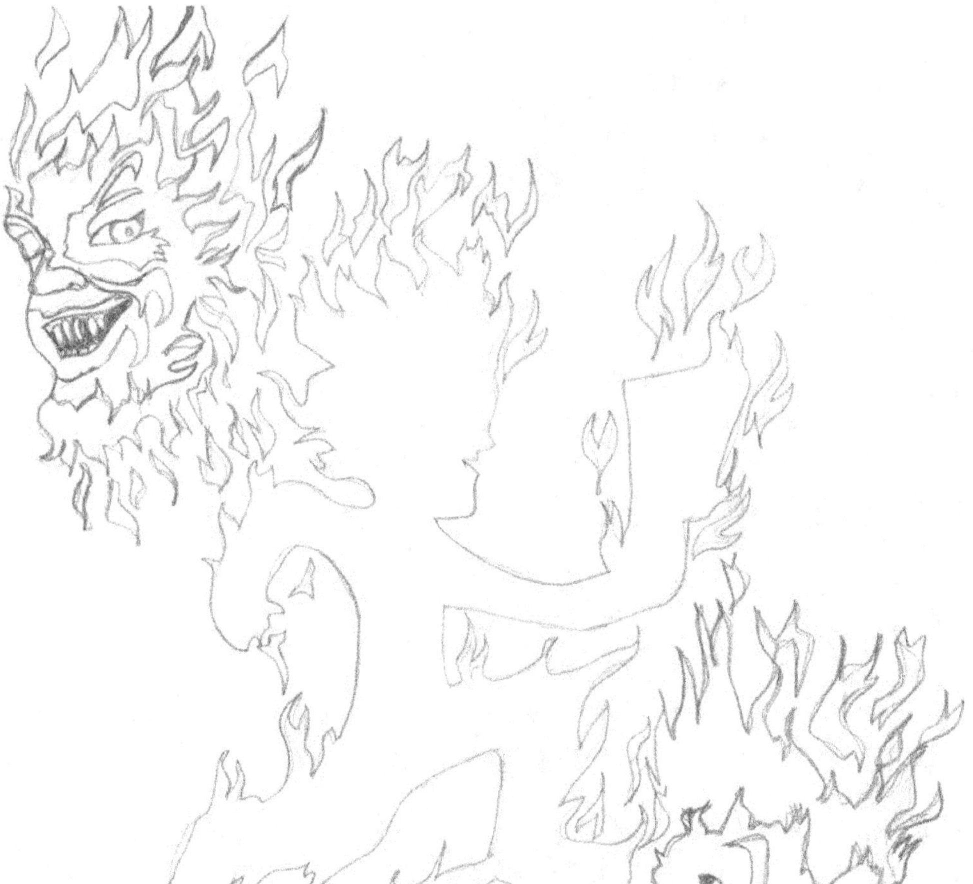

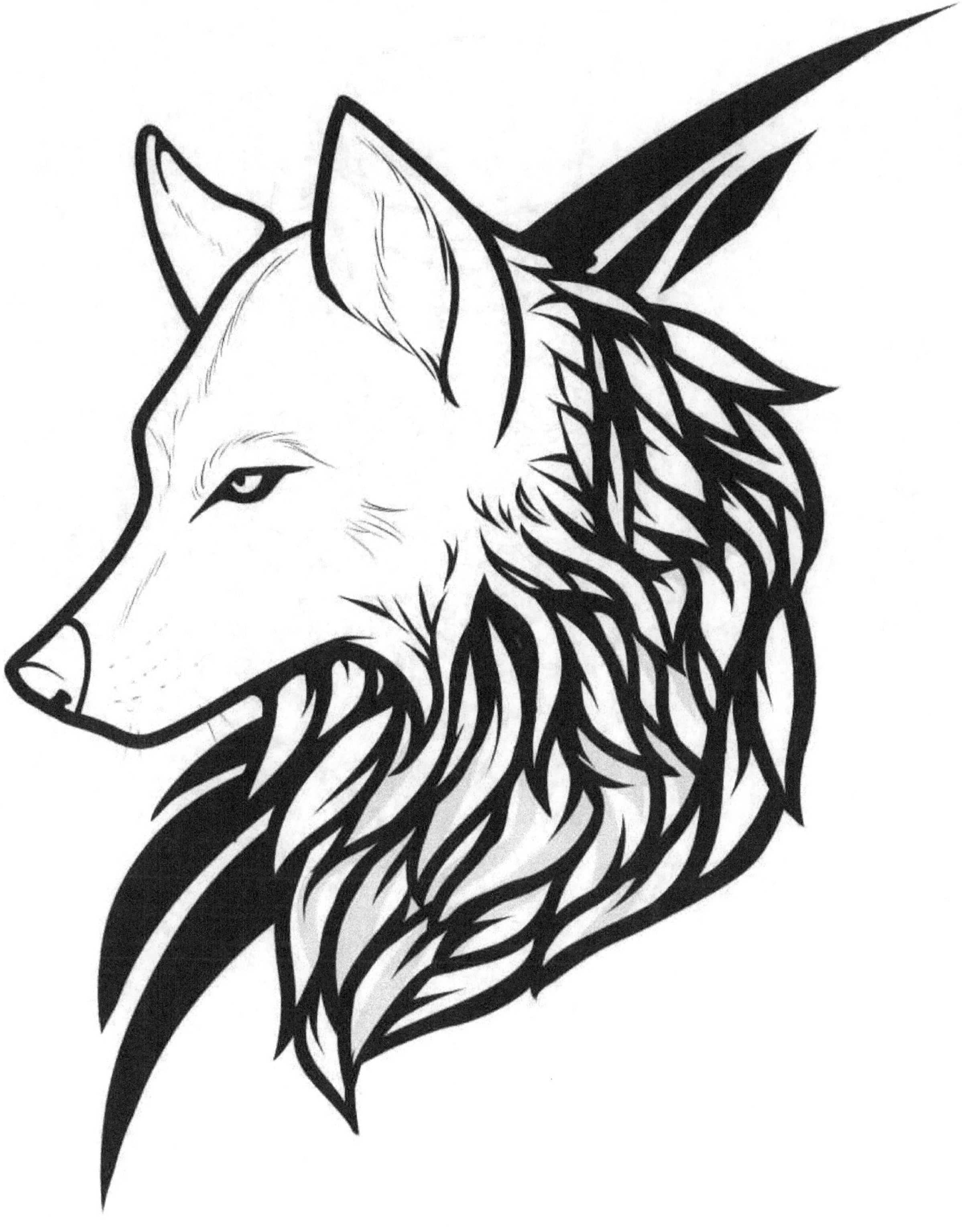

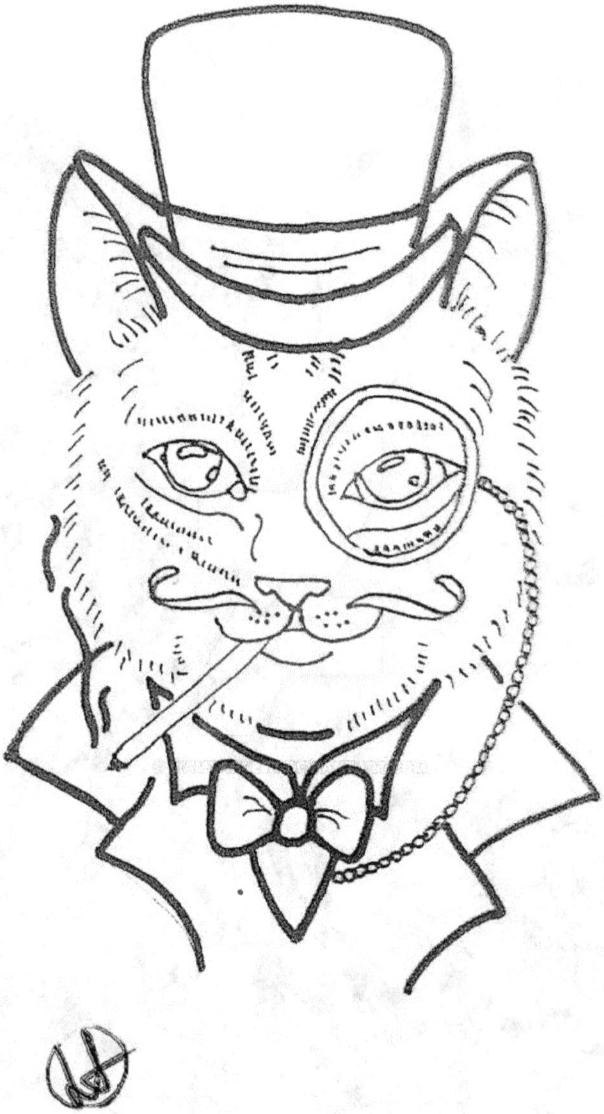

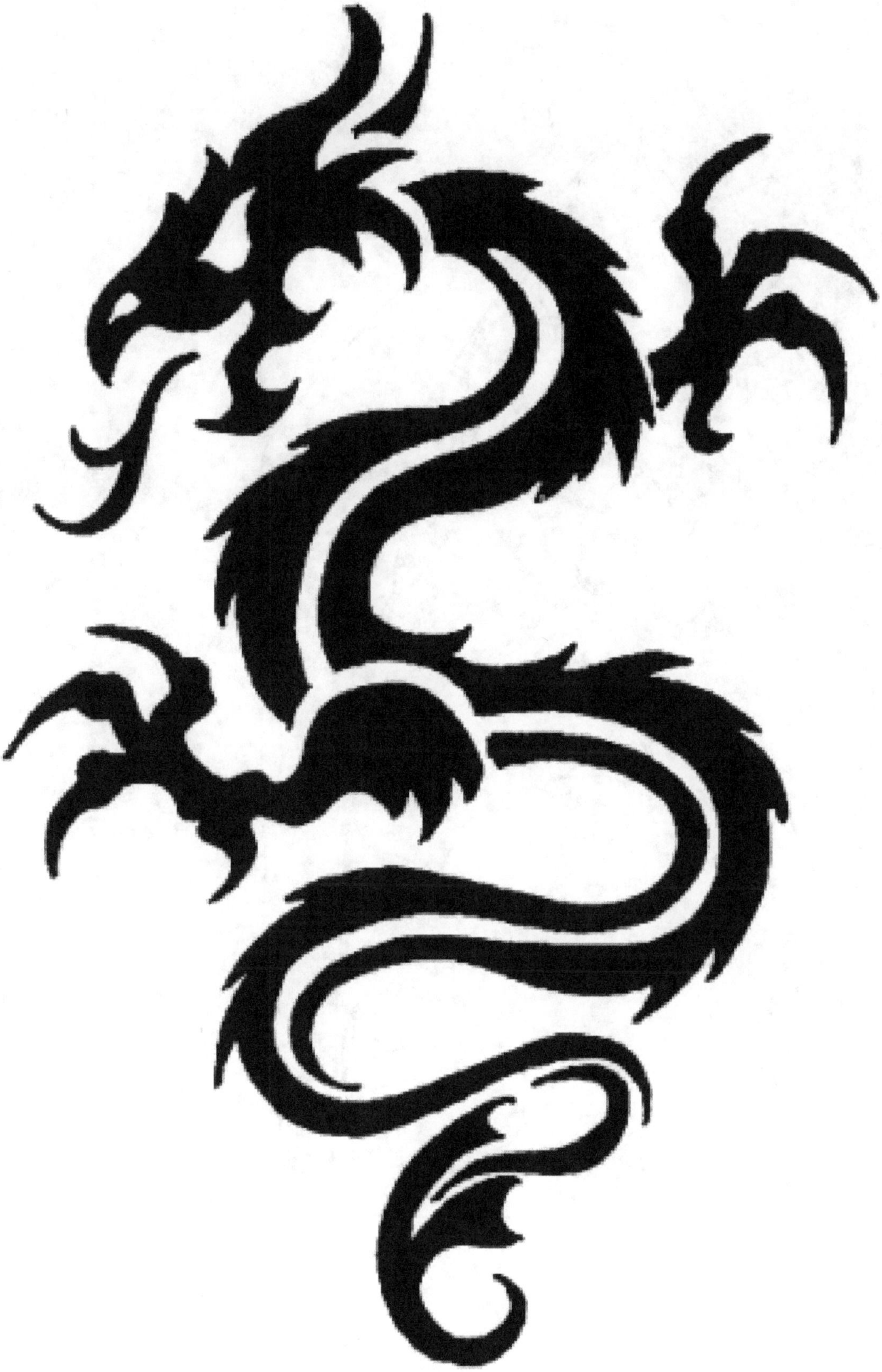

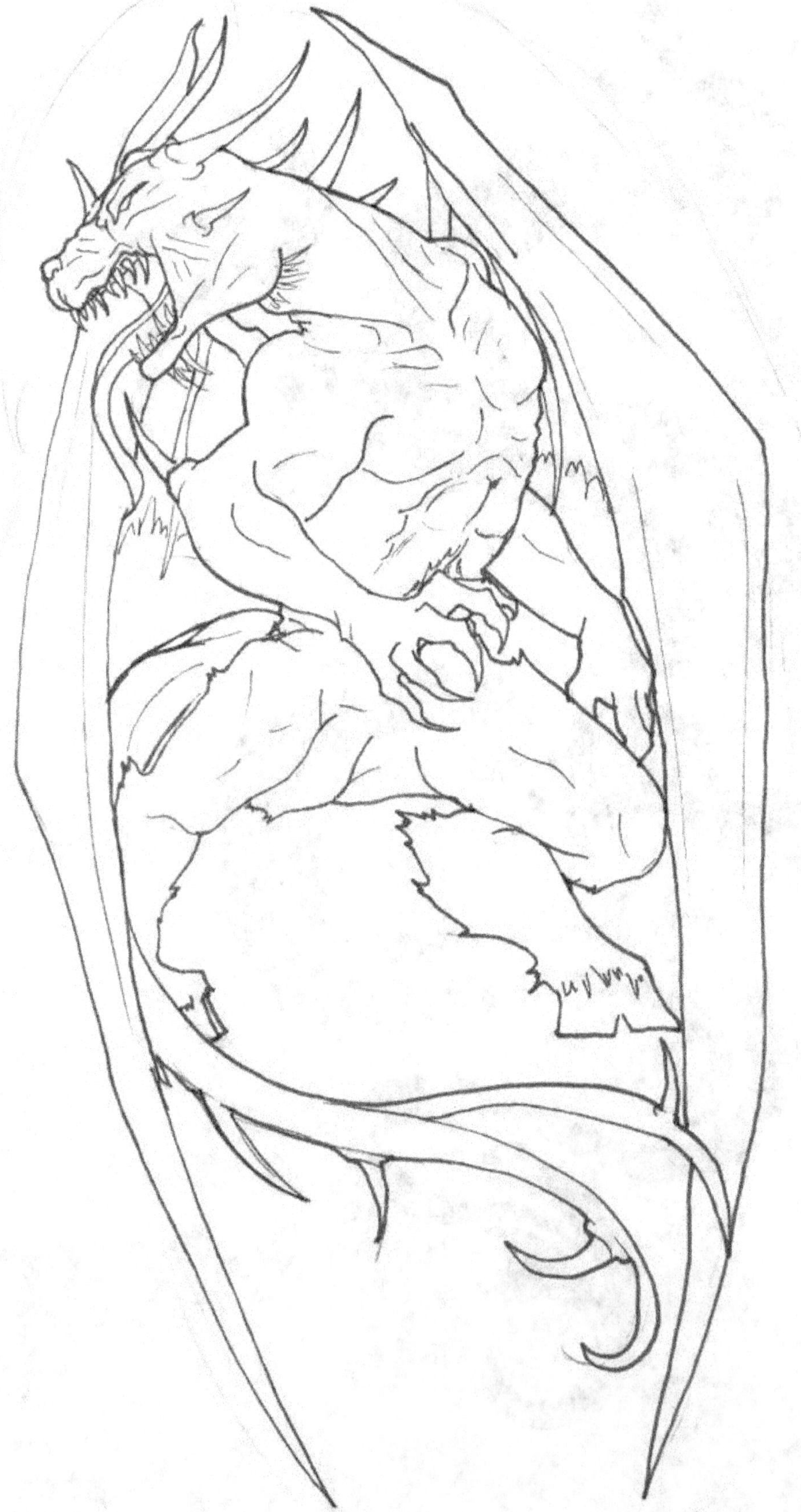

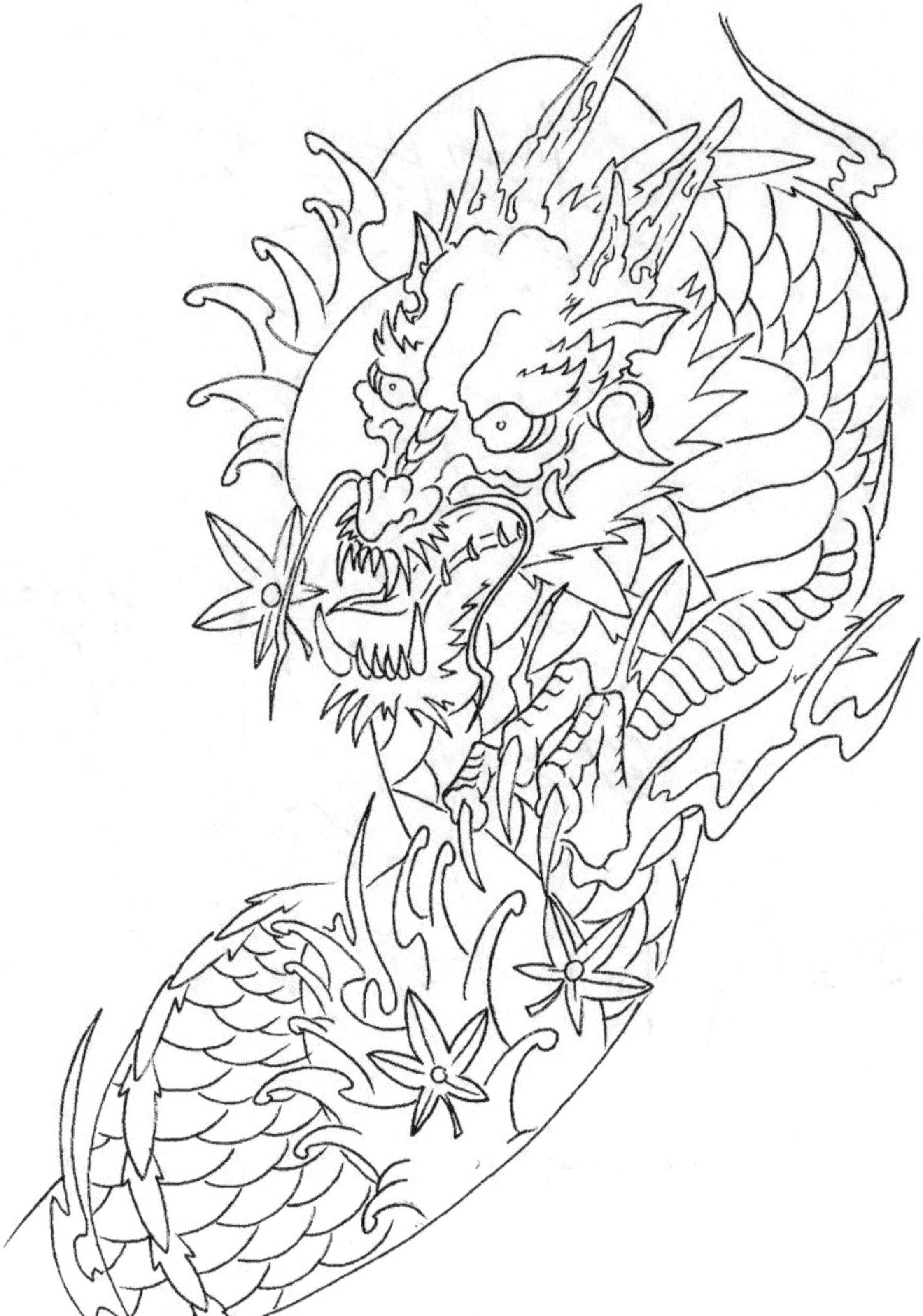

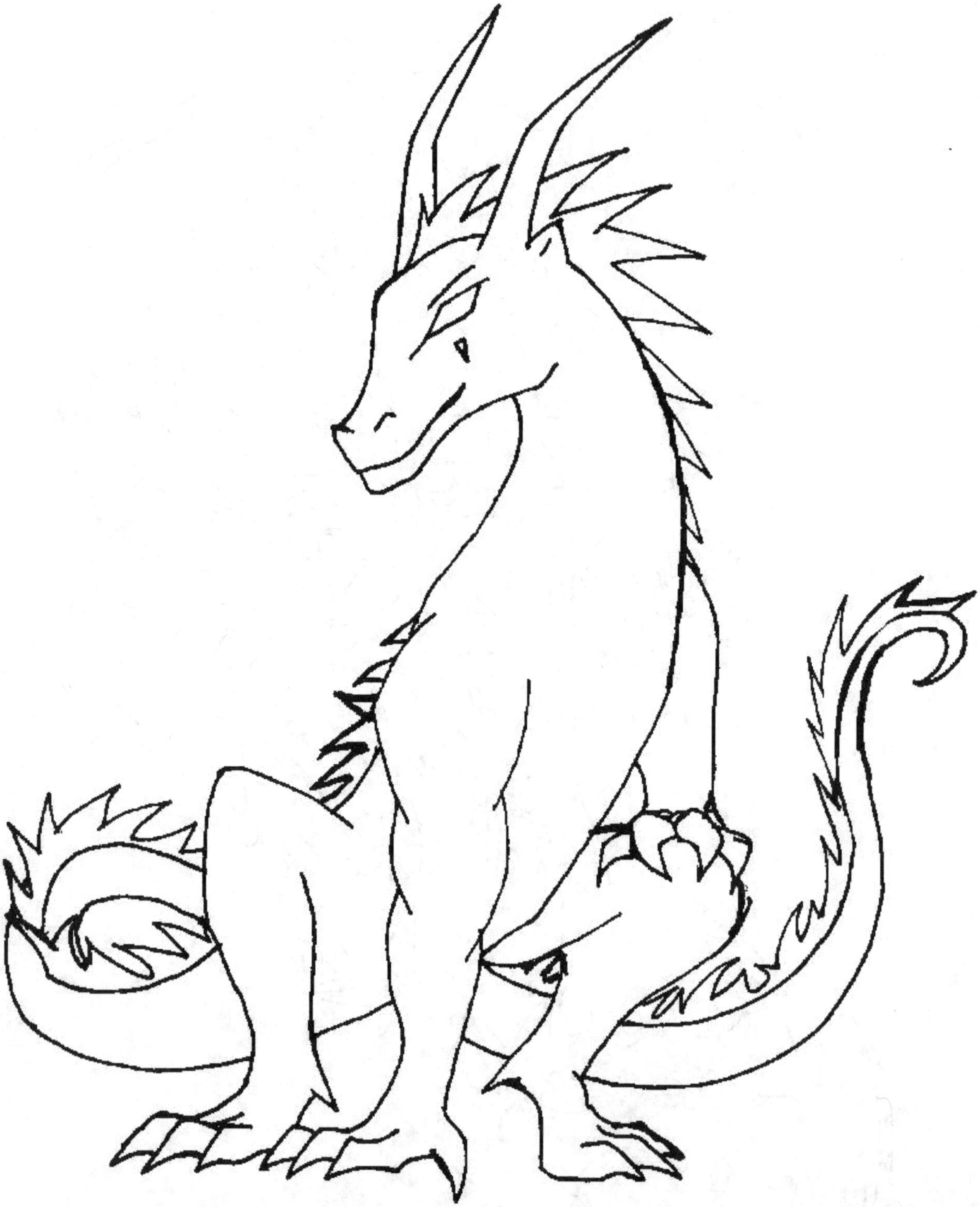

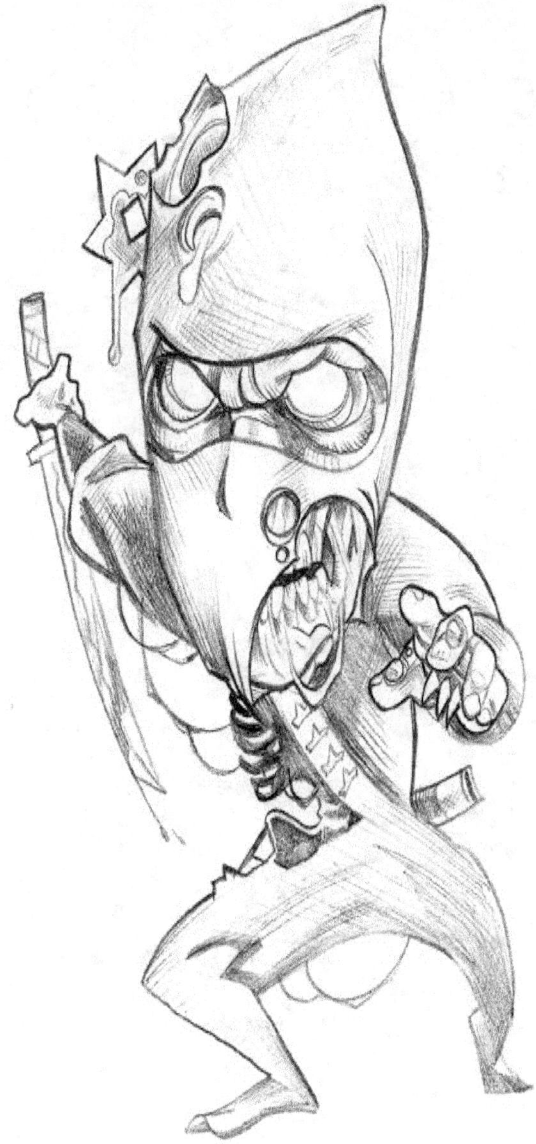

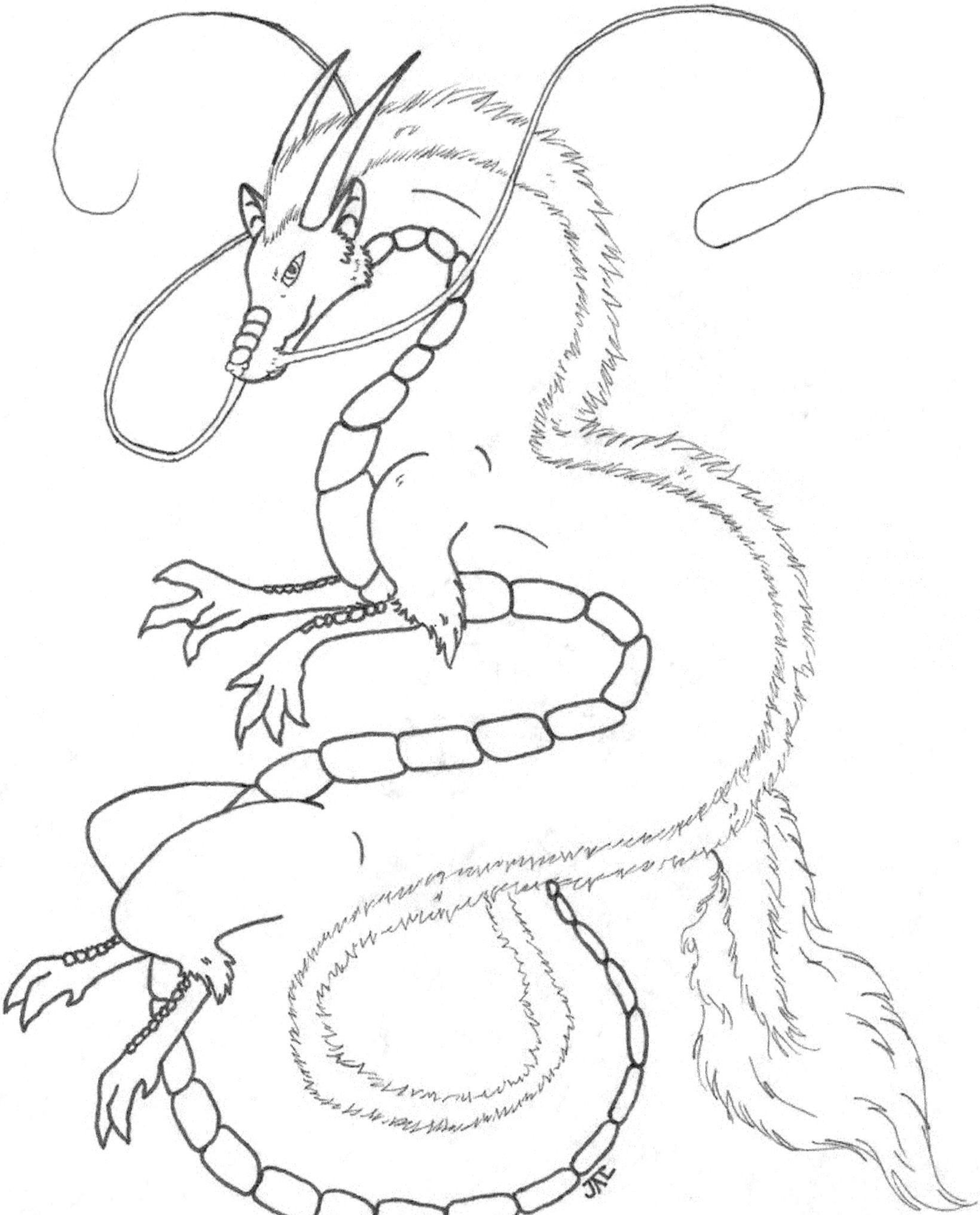

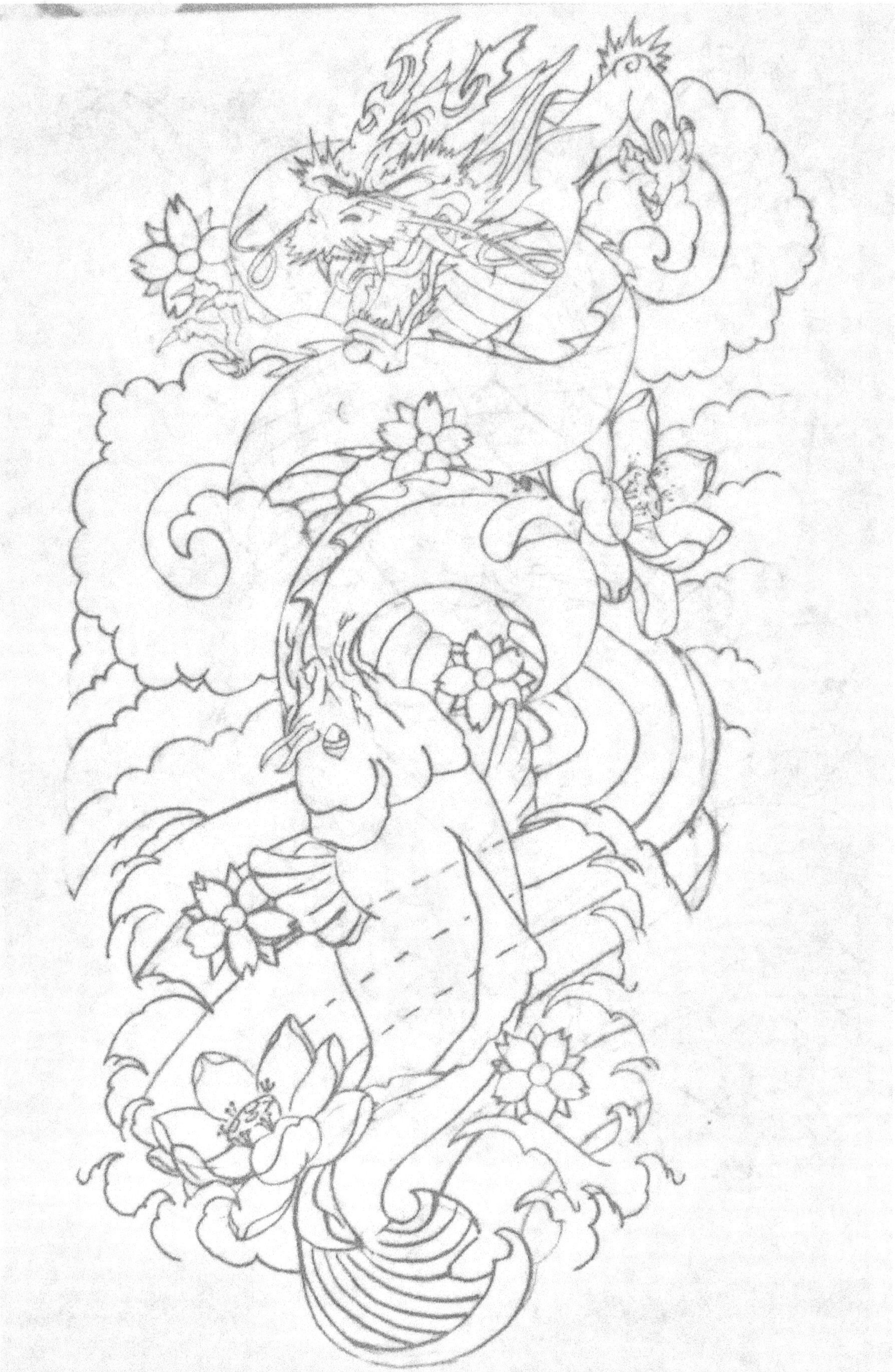

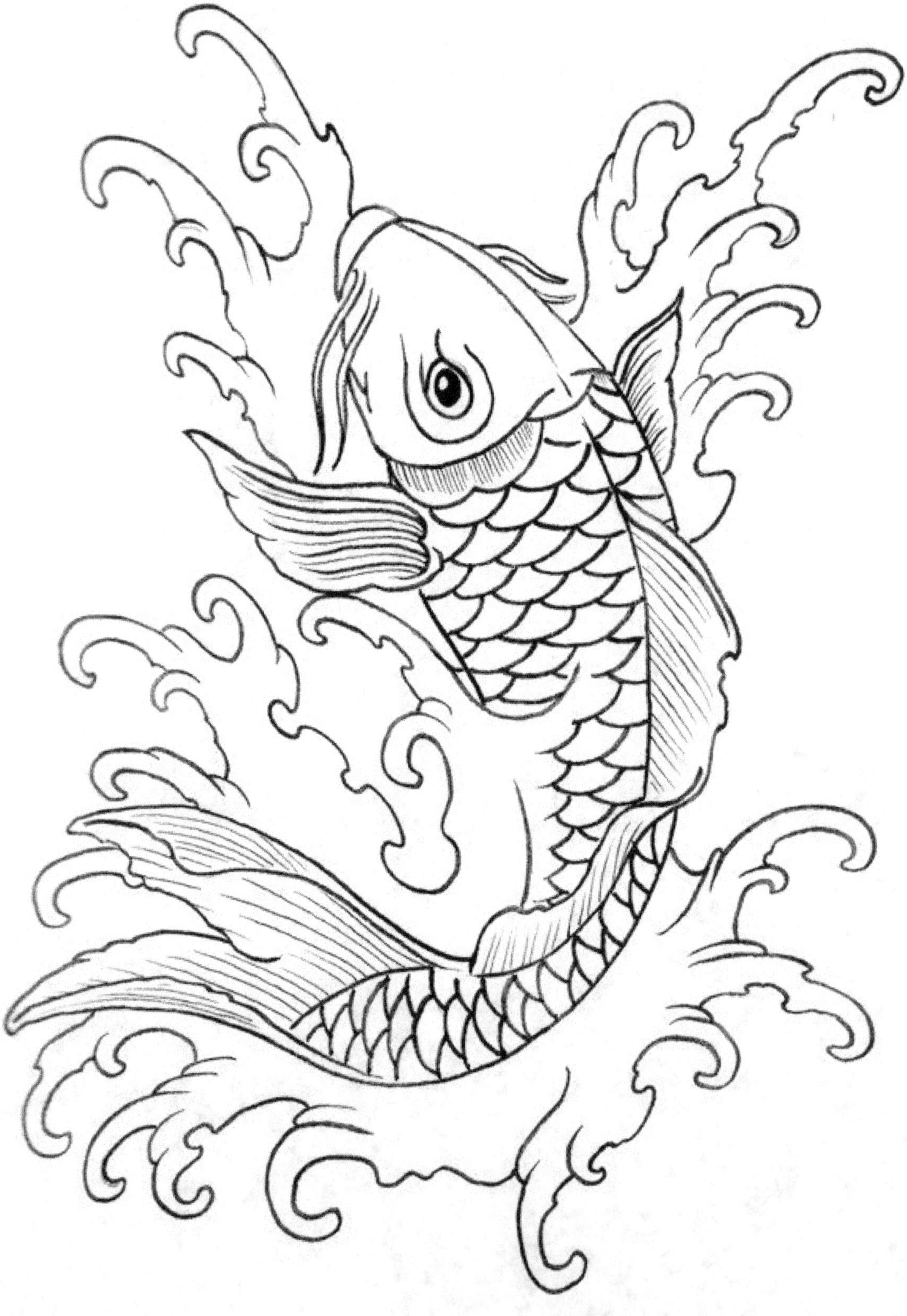

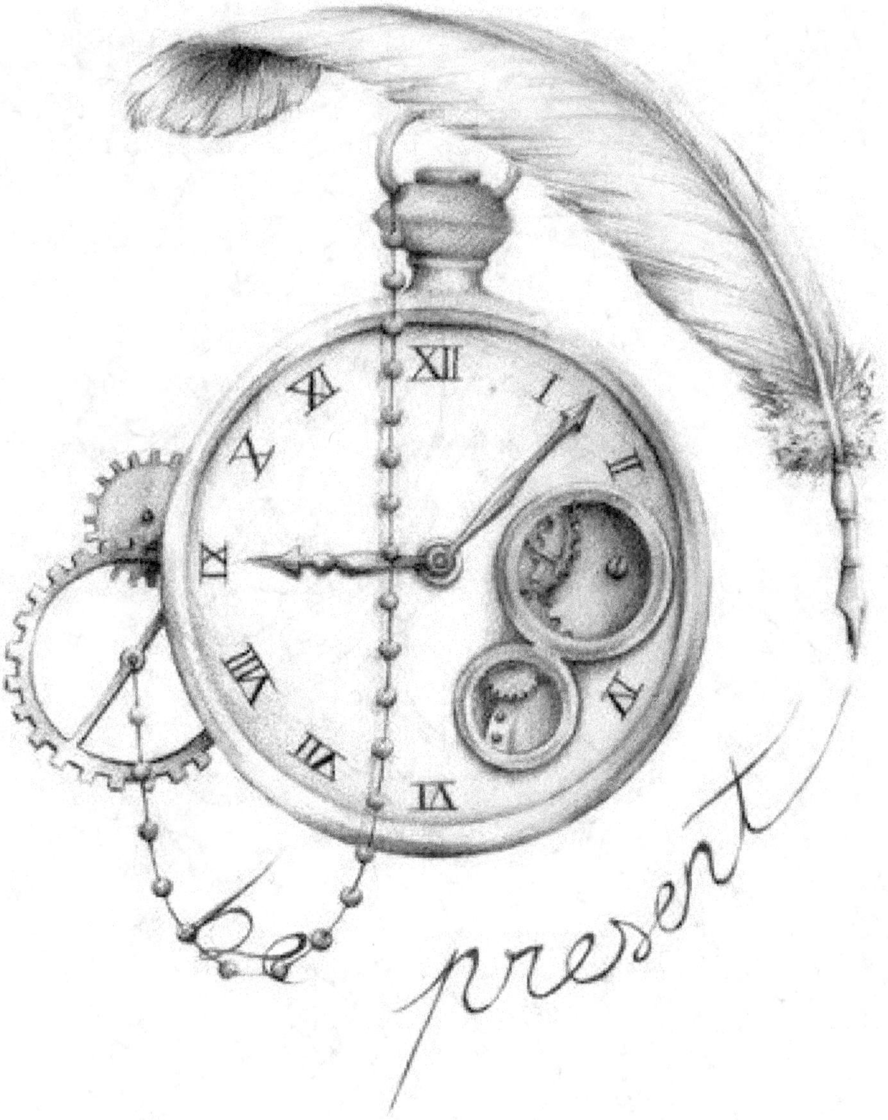
be present

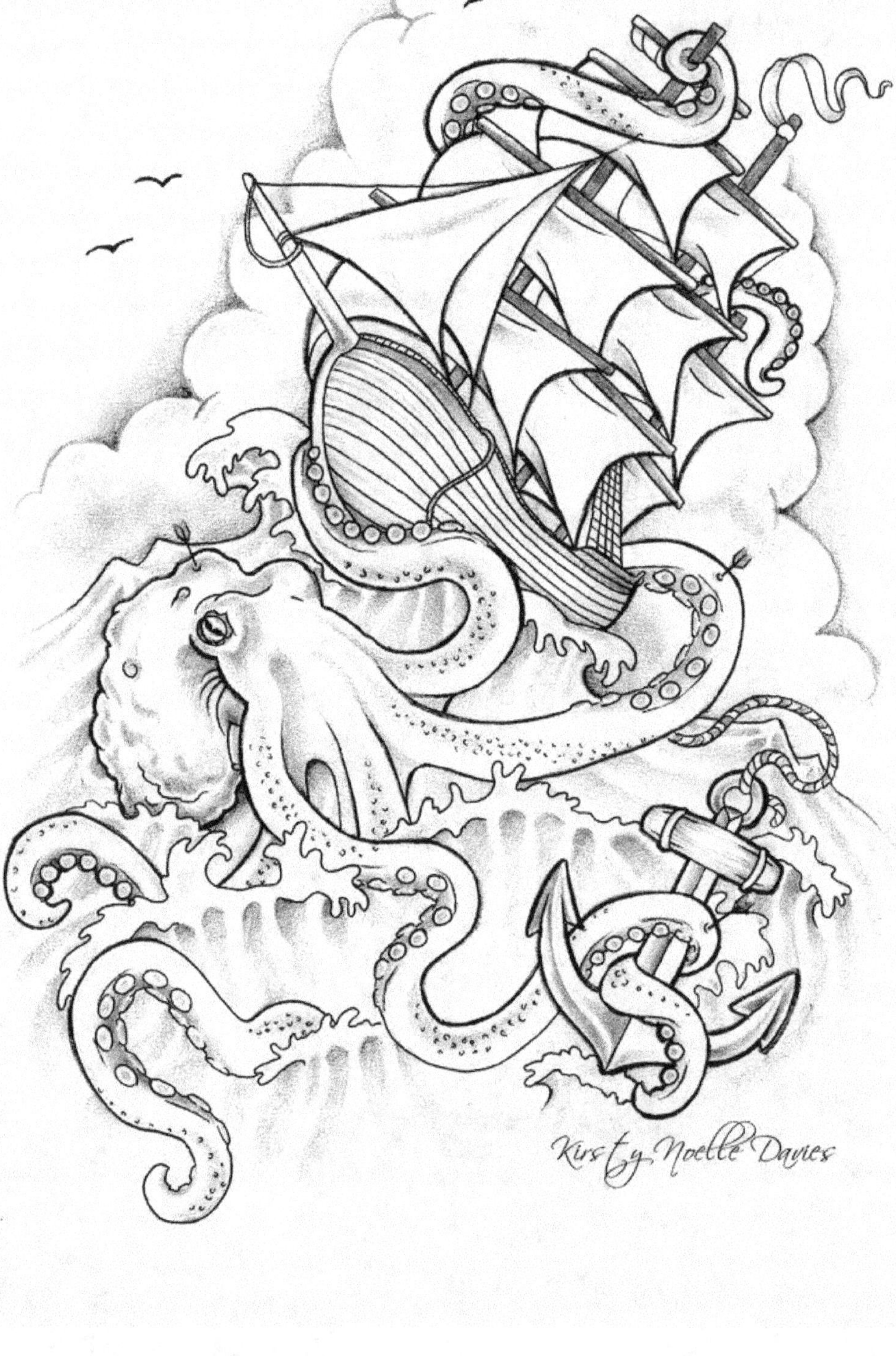
Kirsty Noelle Davies

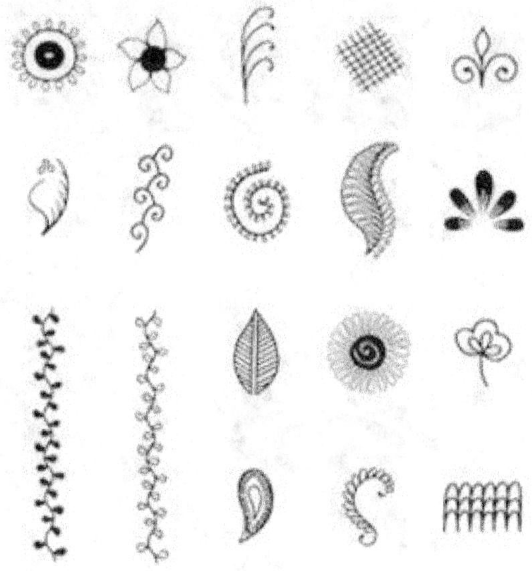

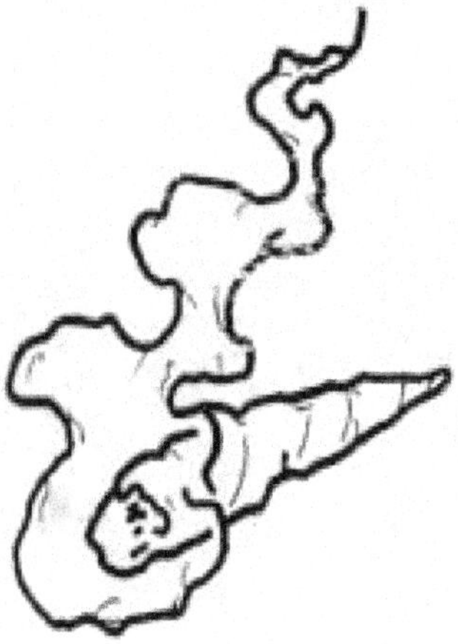

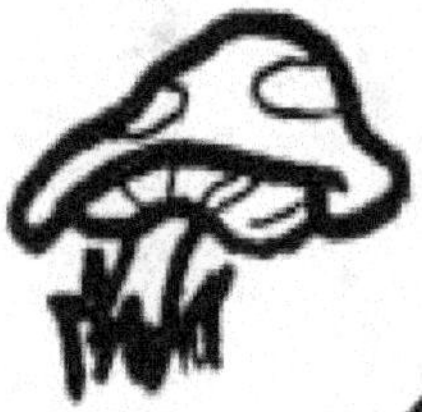

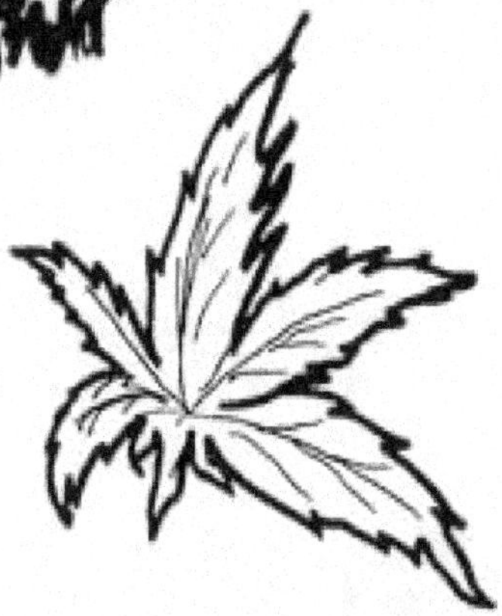

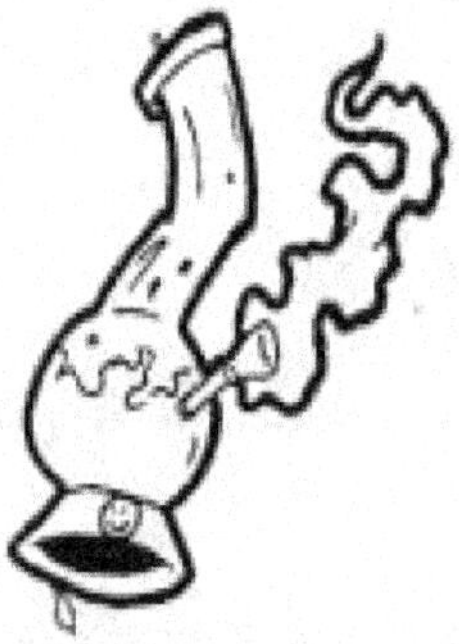

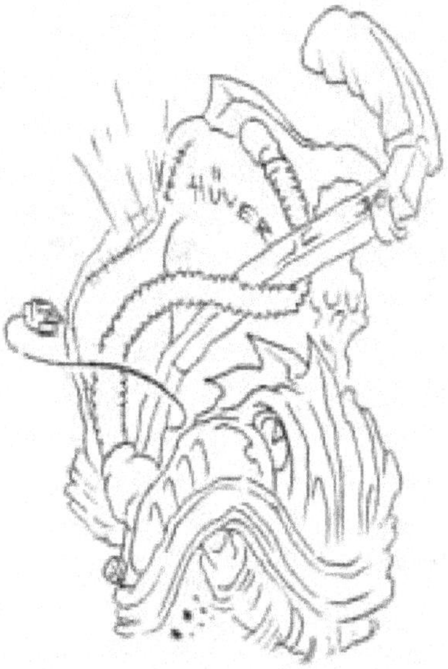

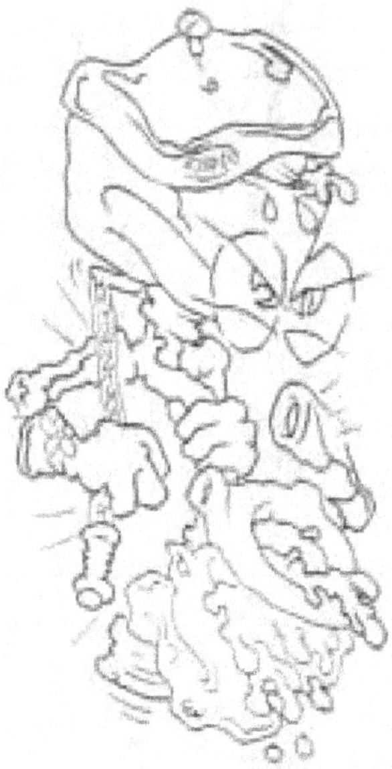

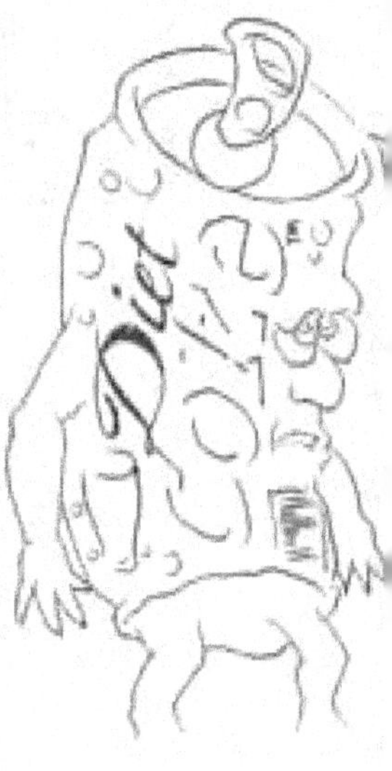
Diet

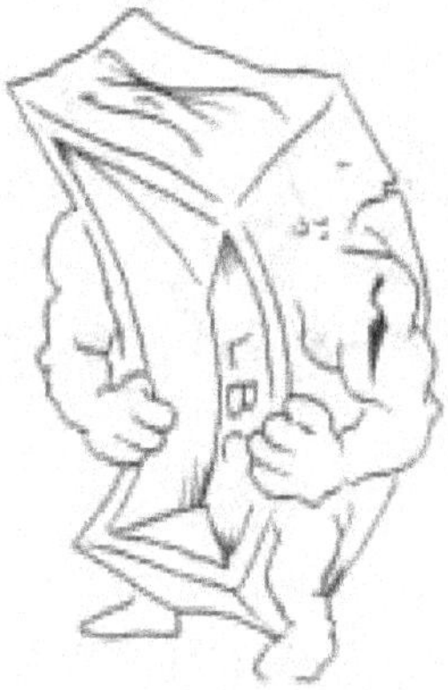

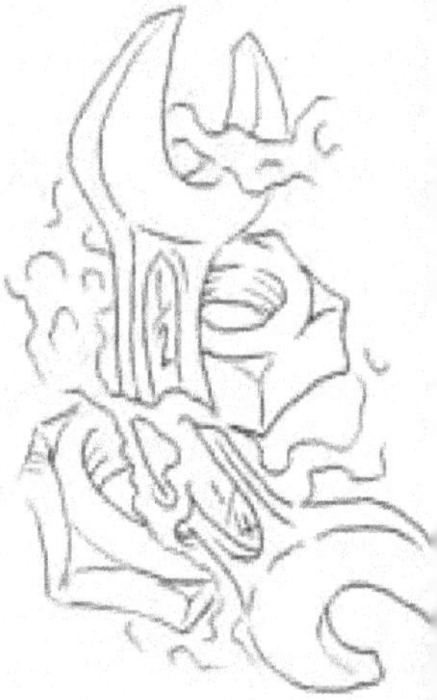

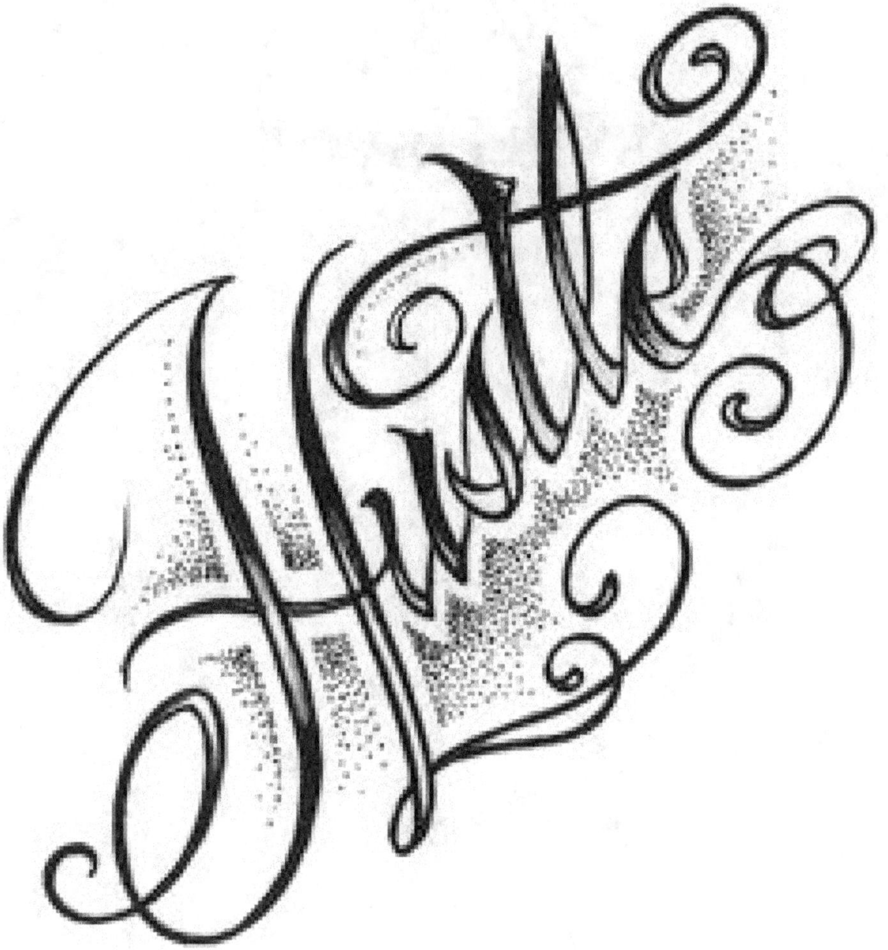
Hustle

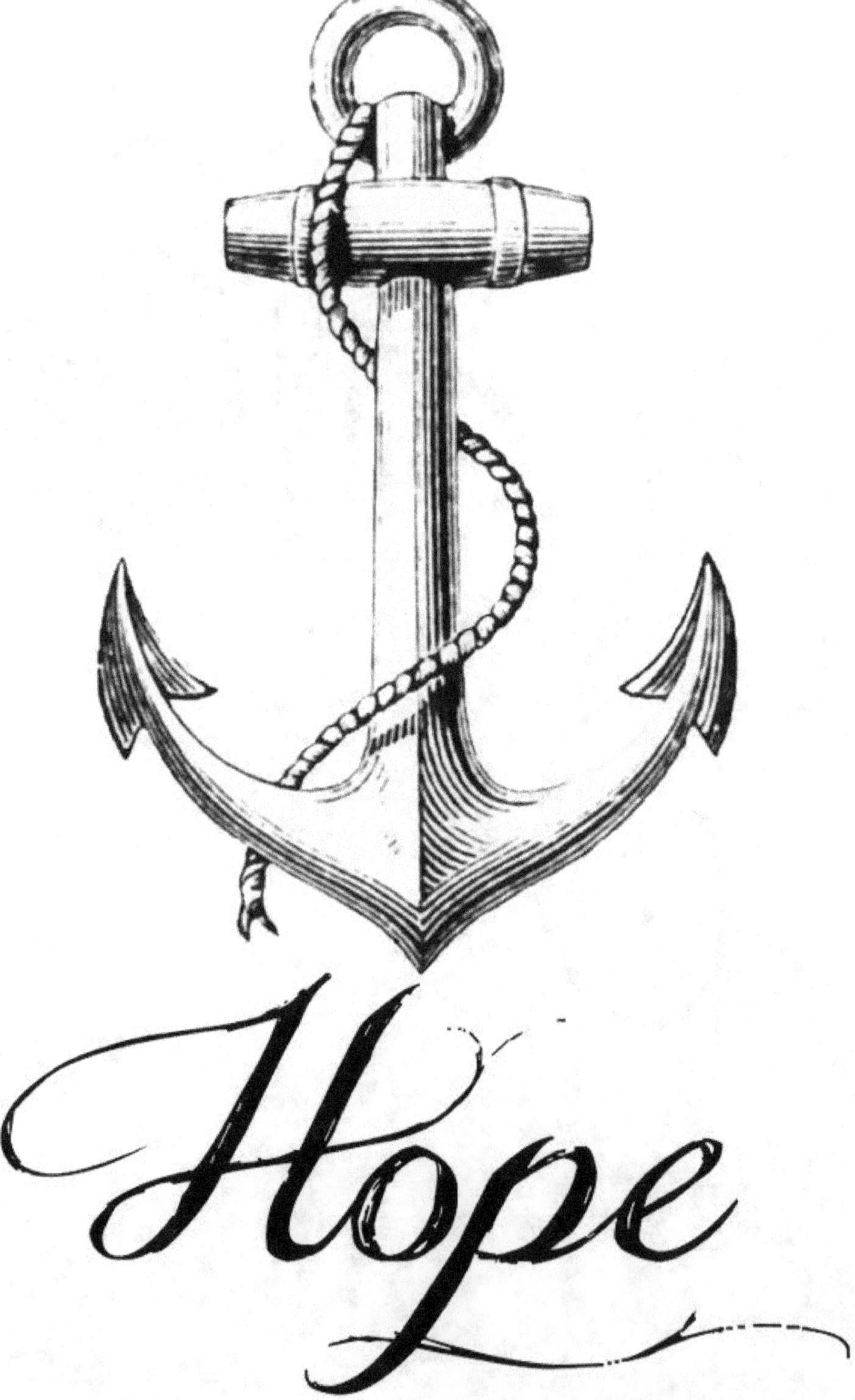
Hope

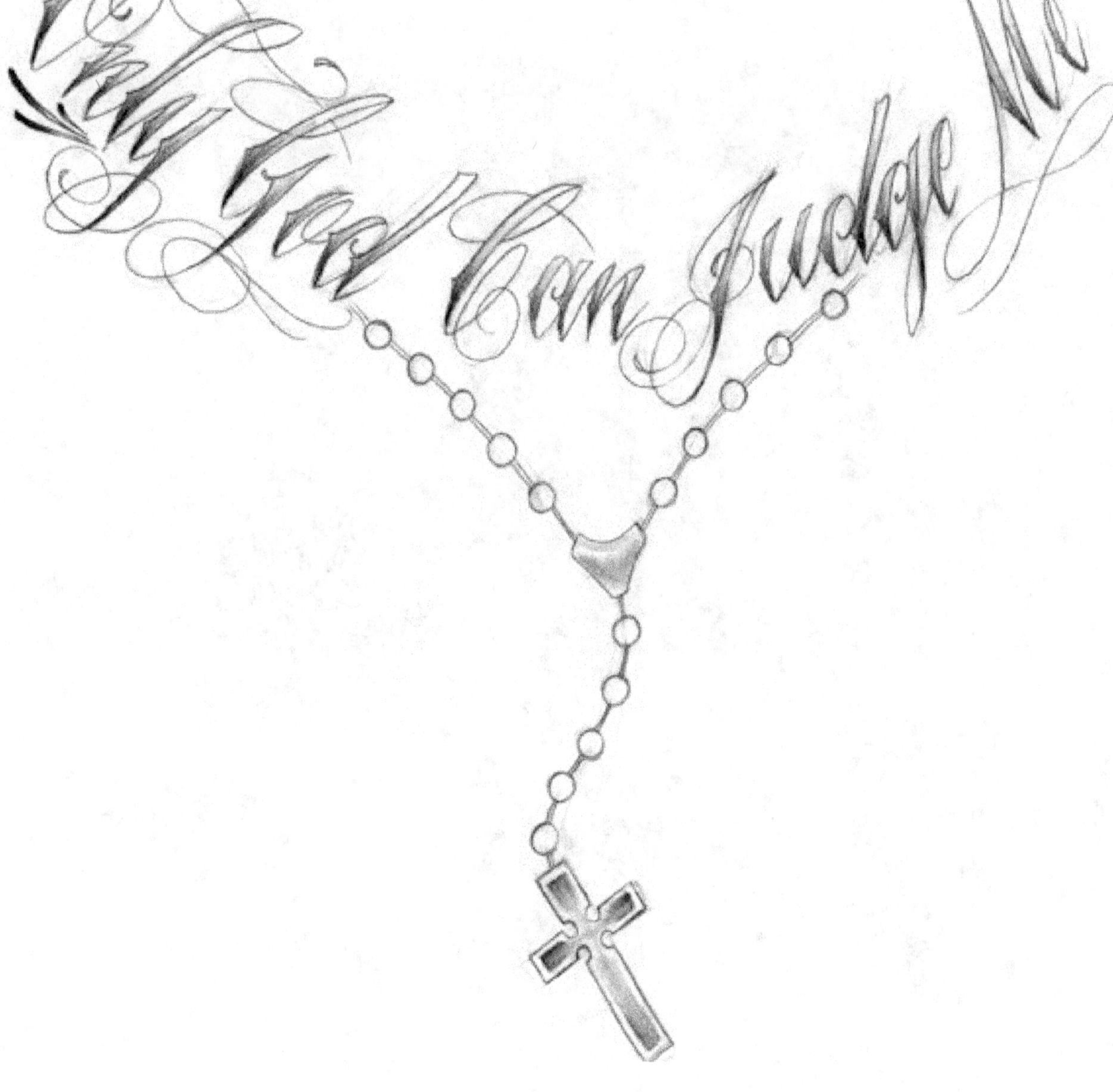
Only God Can Judge Me

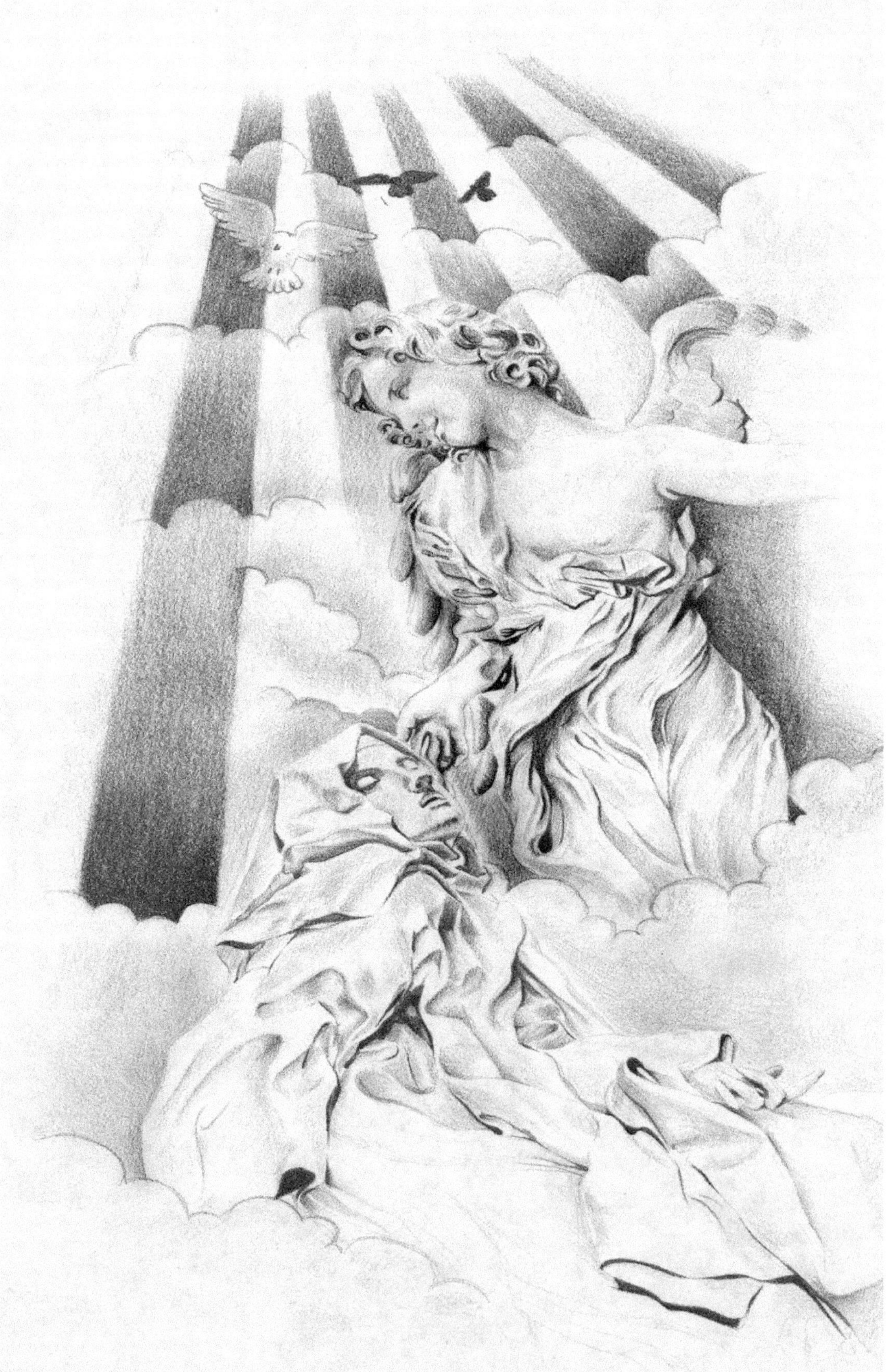

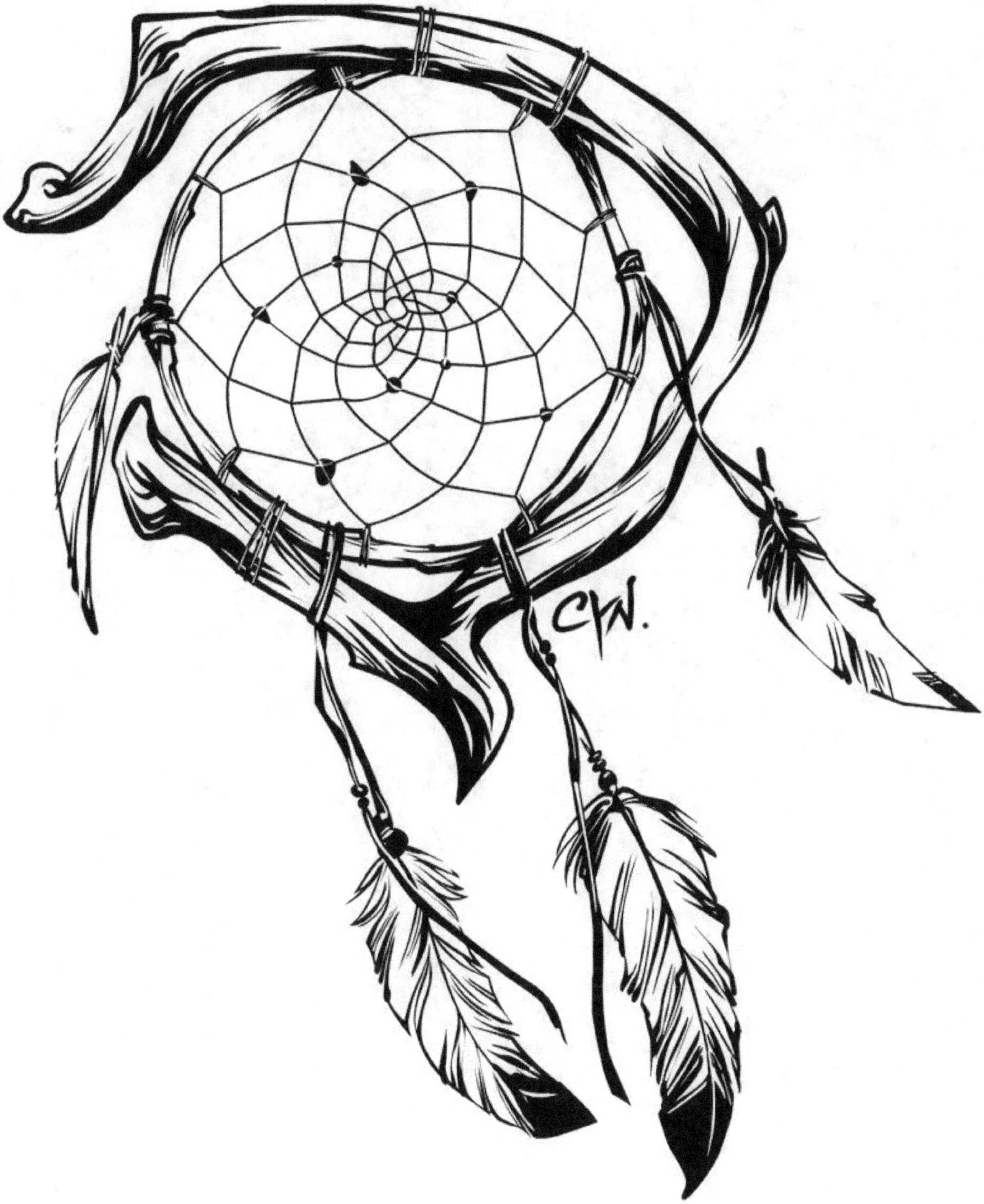
CW.

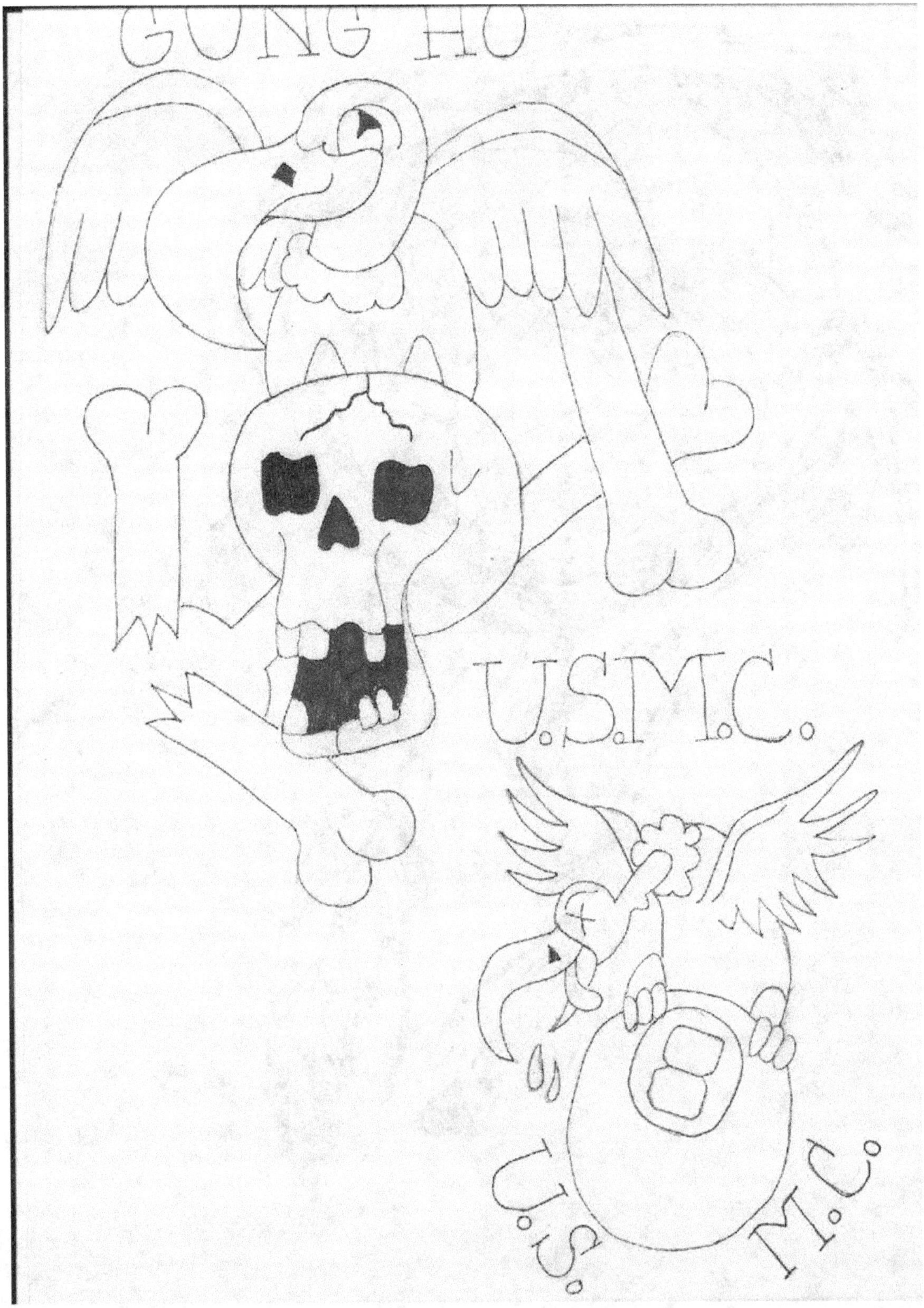
GONG HO
U.S.M.C.
U.S. M.C.

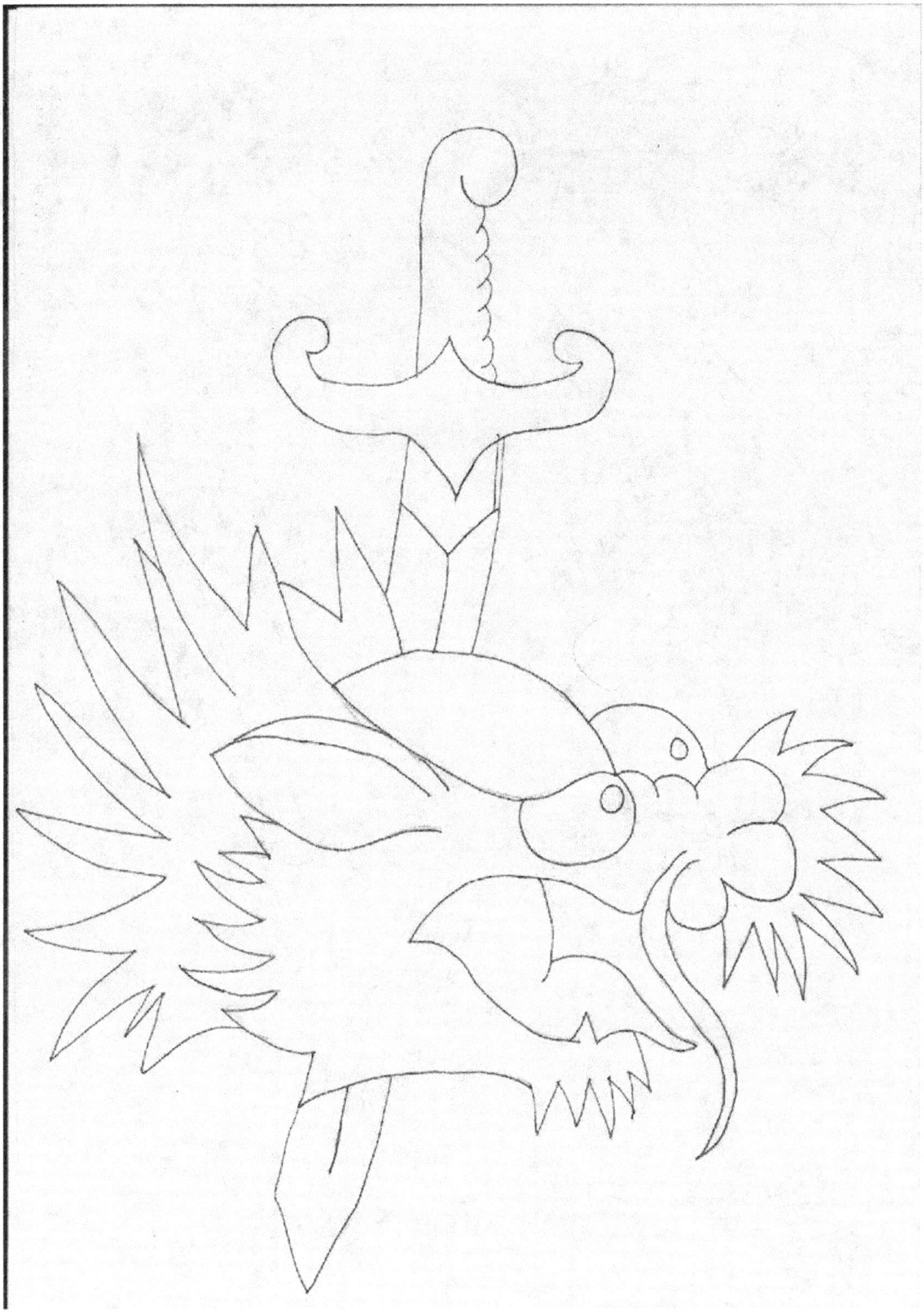

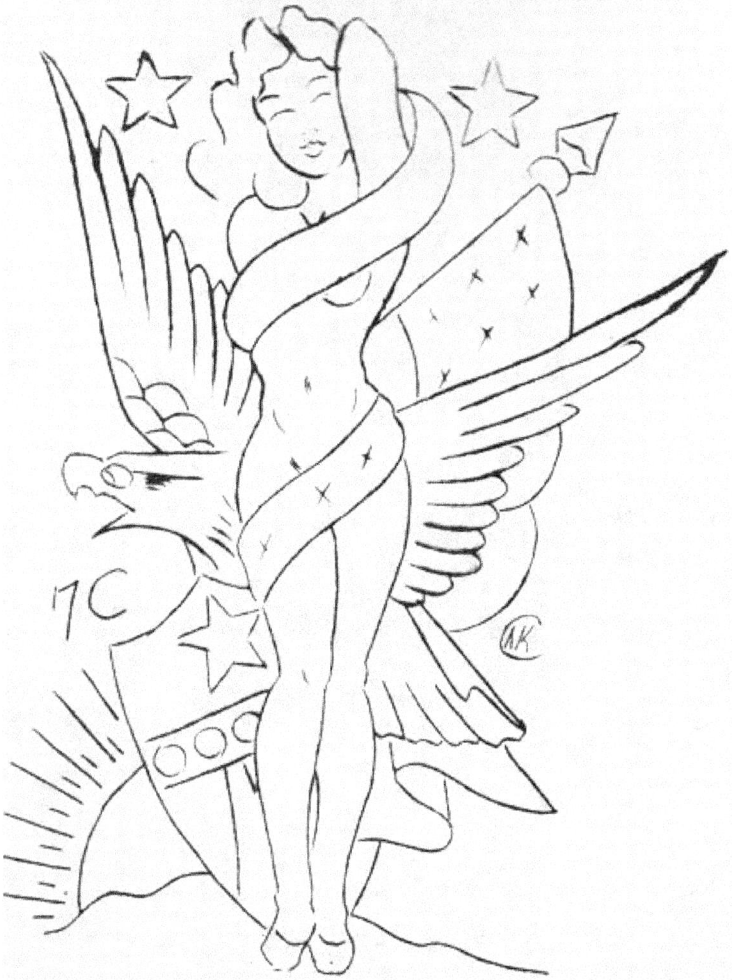

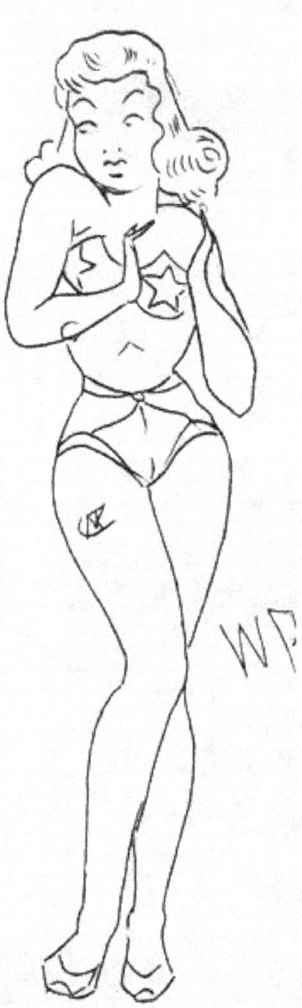

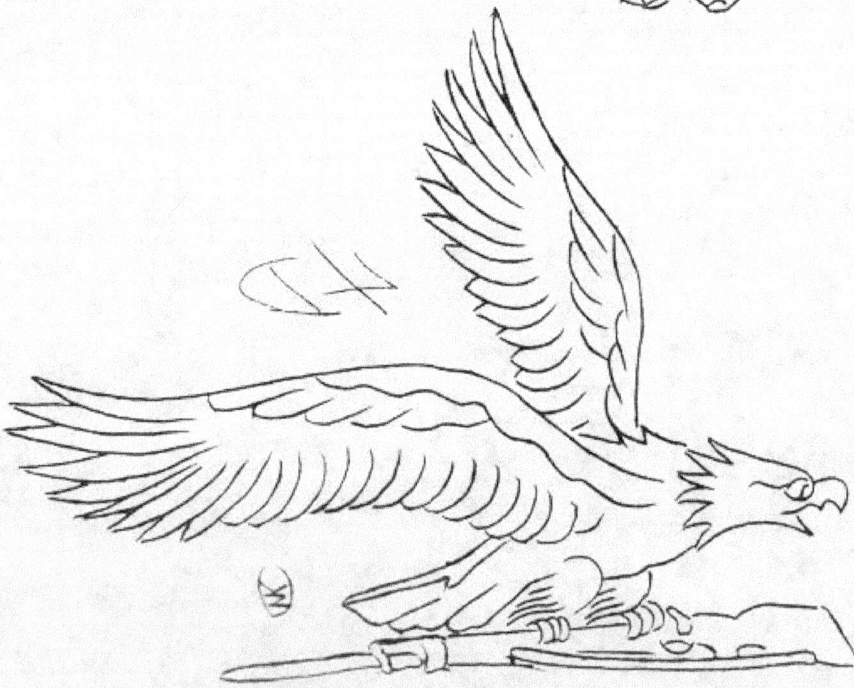

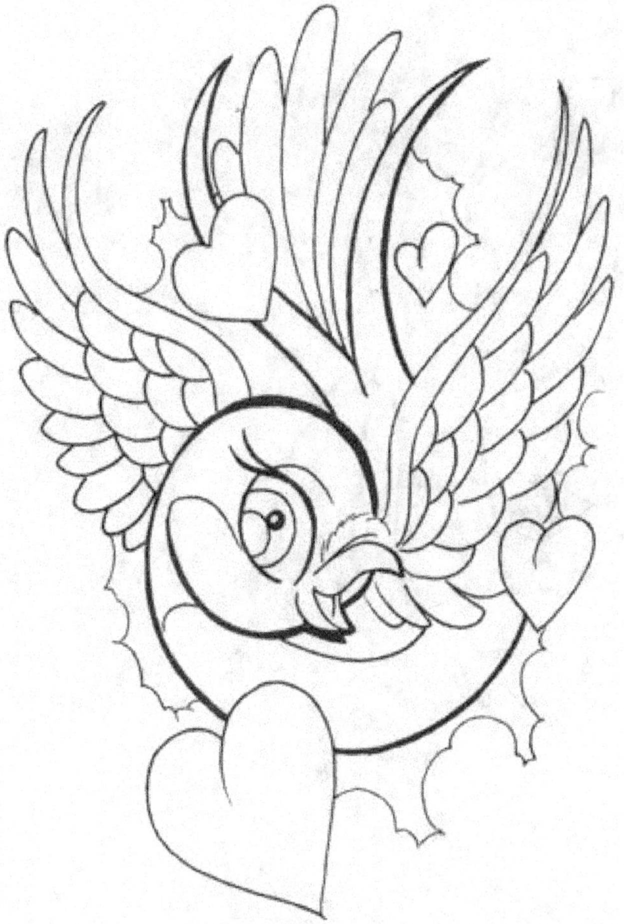

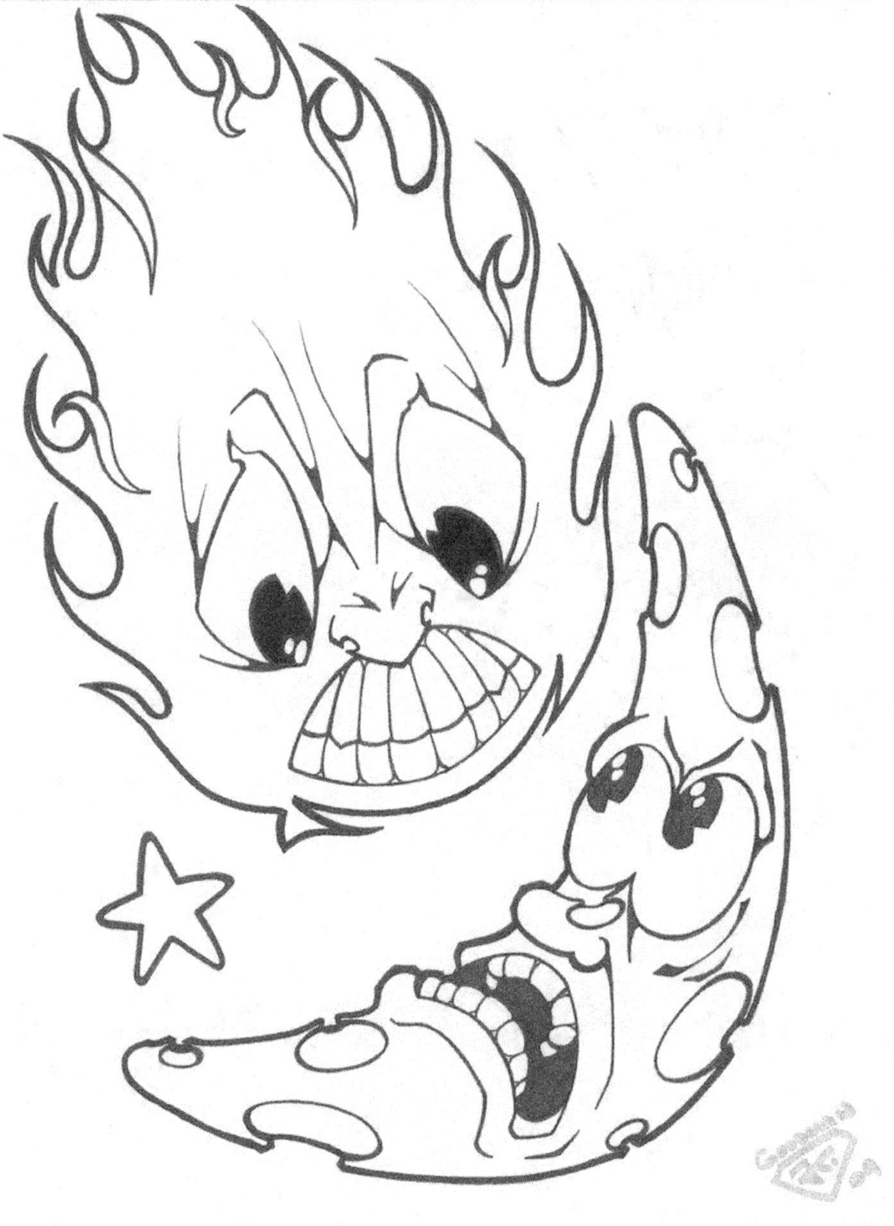

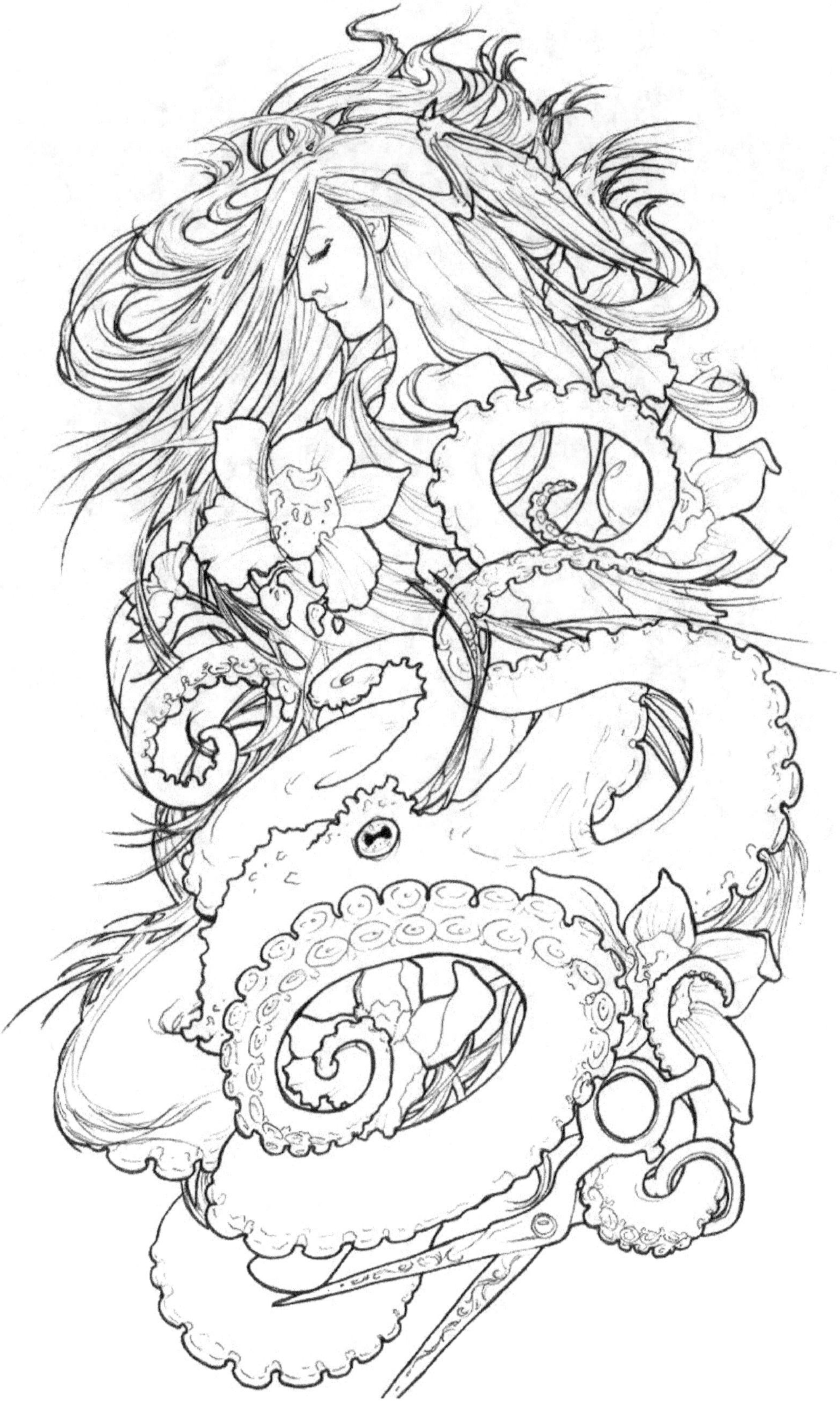

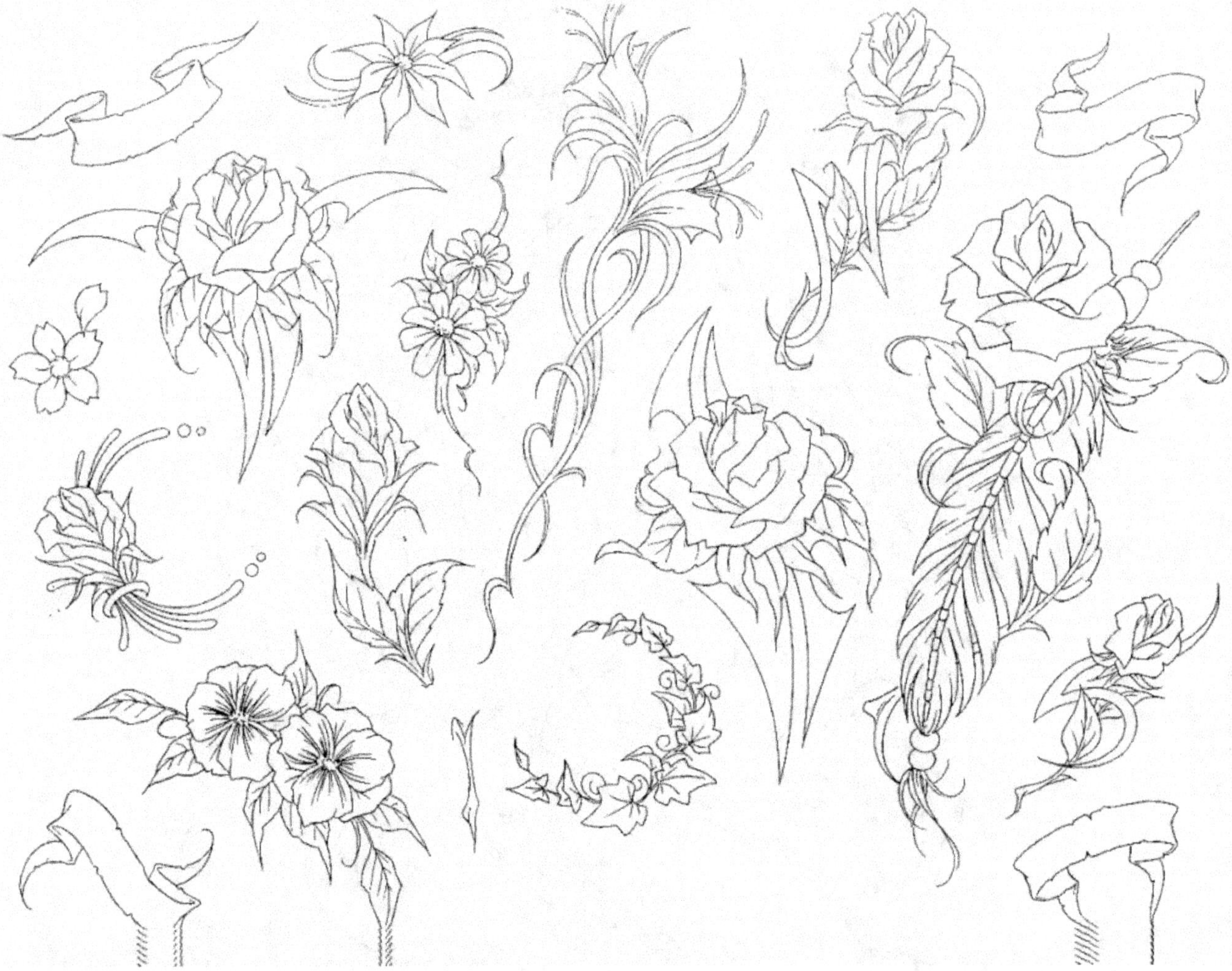

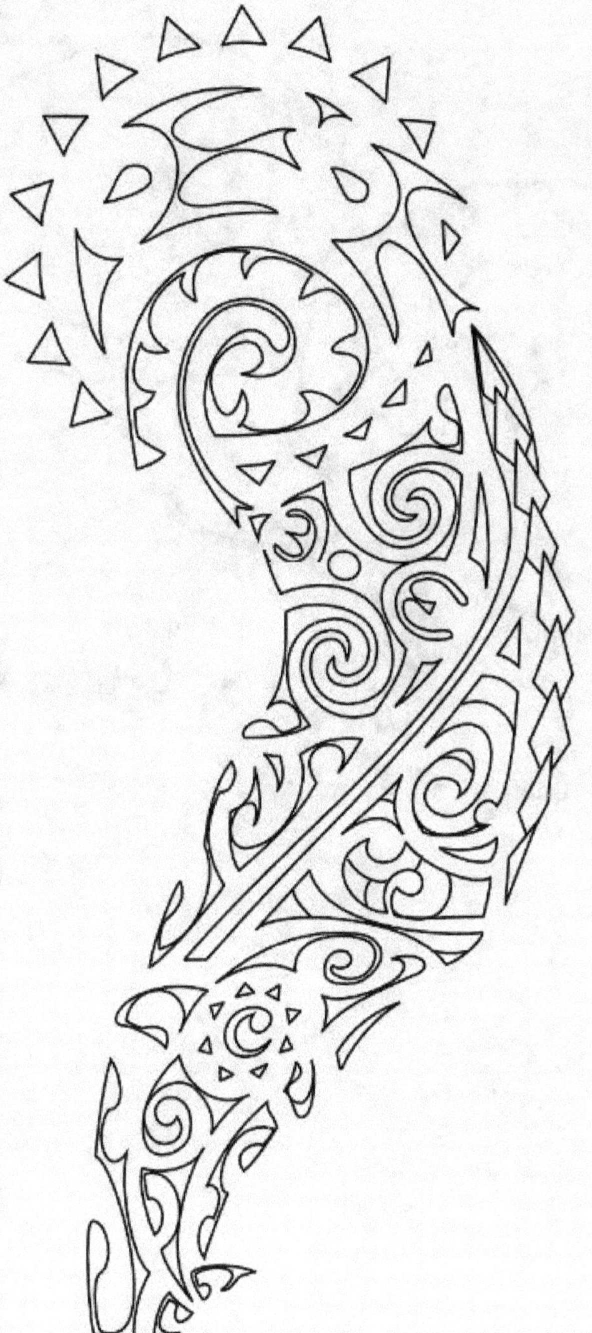

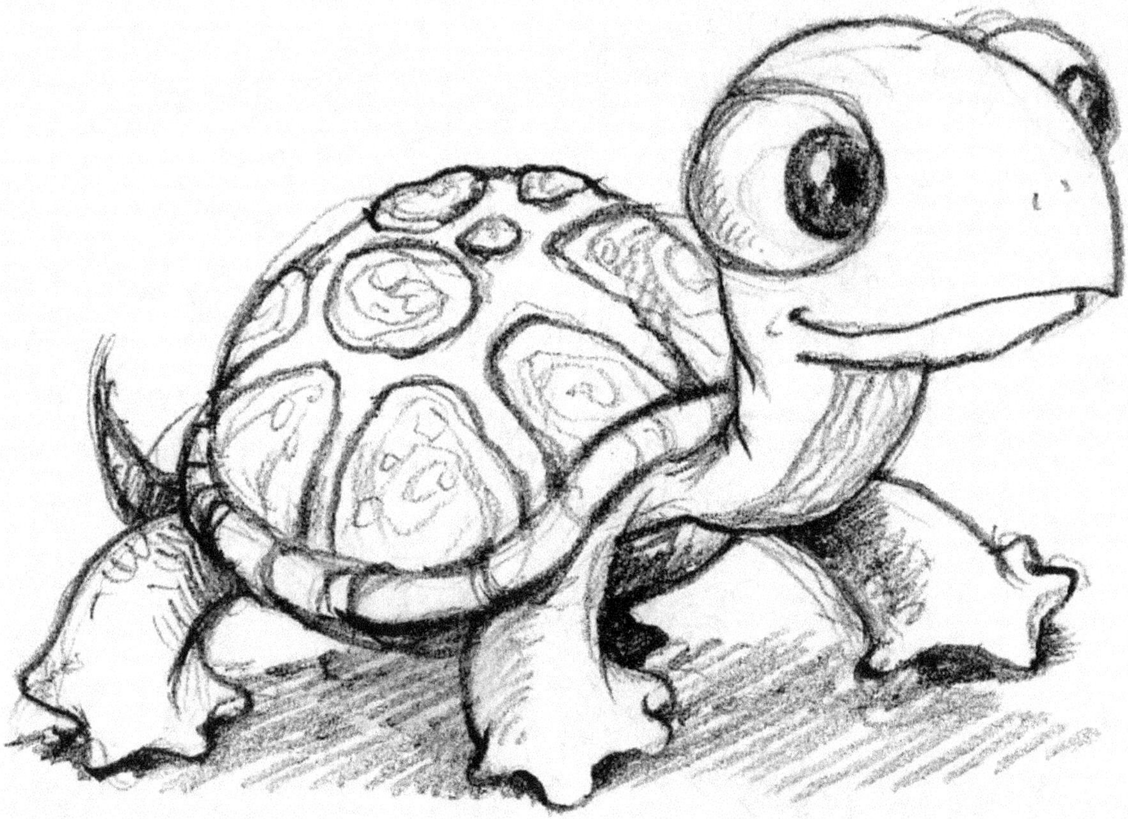

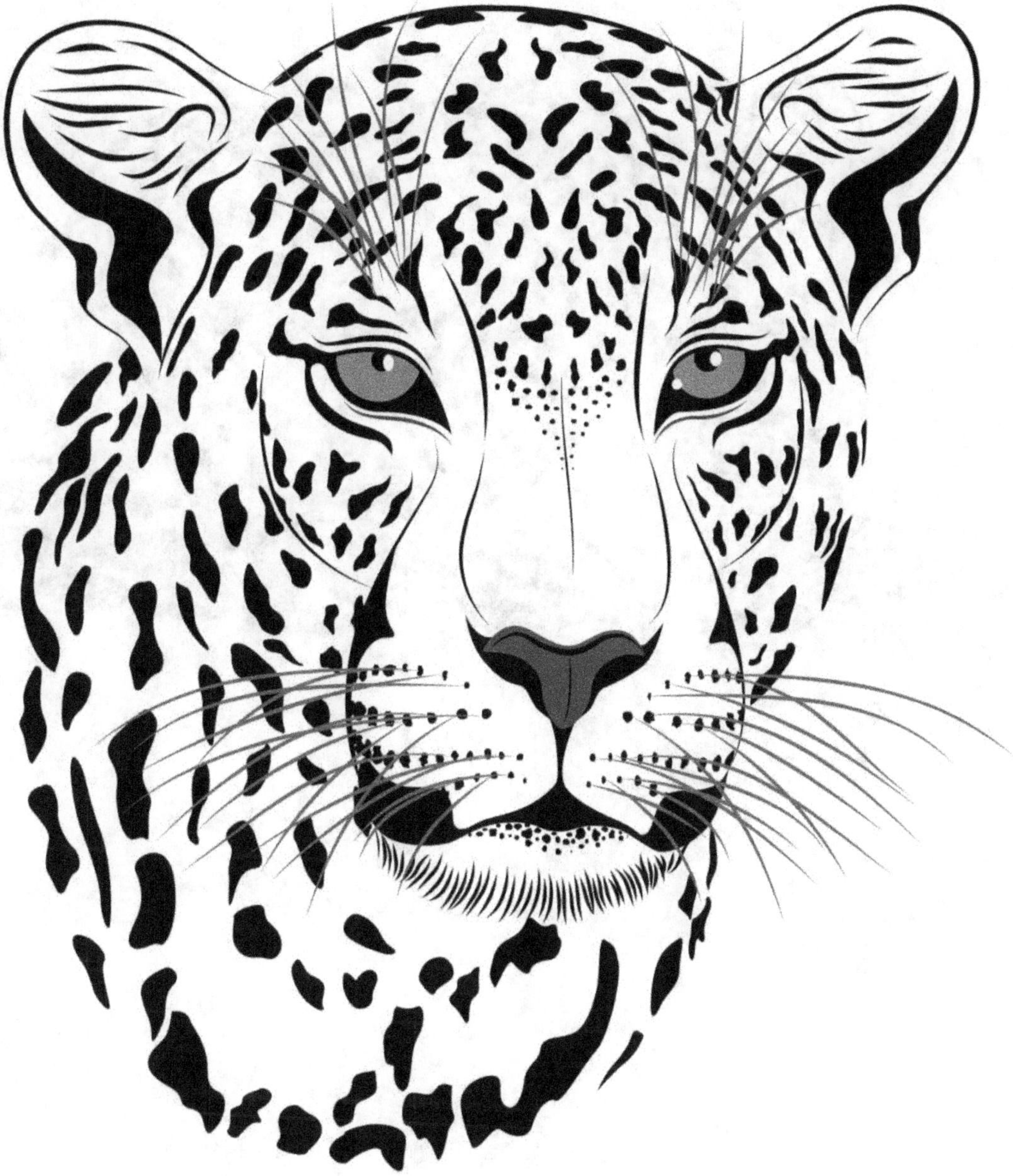

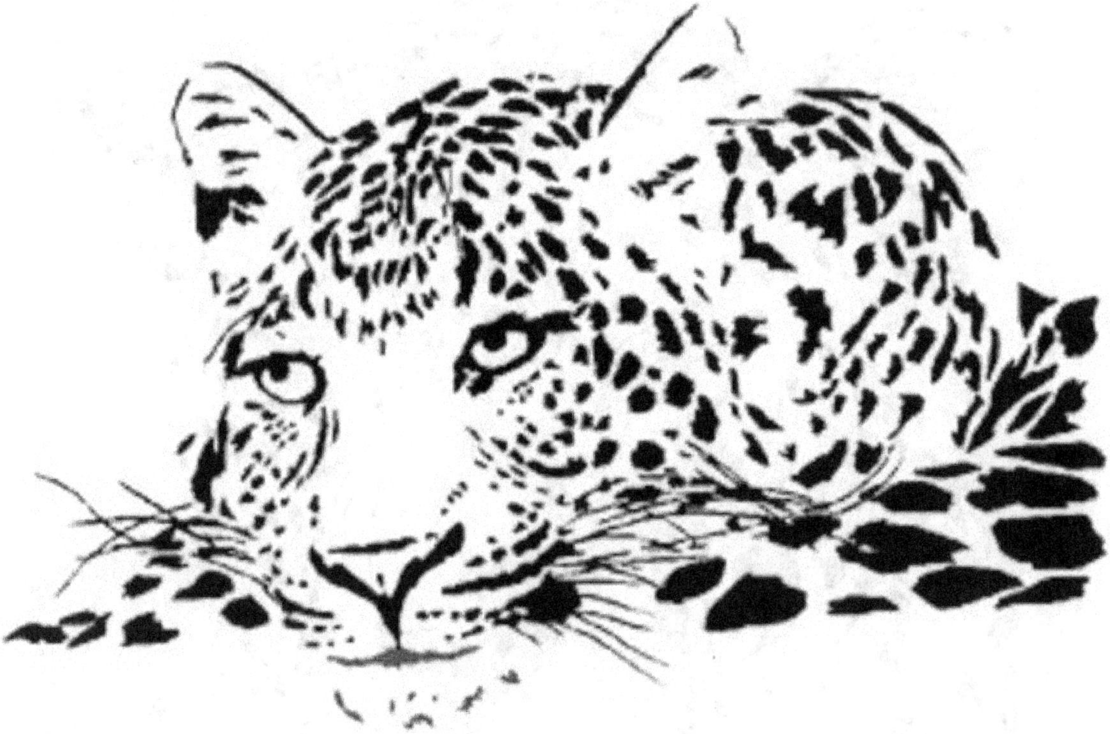

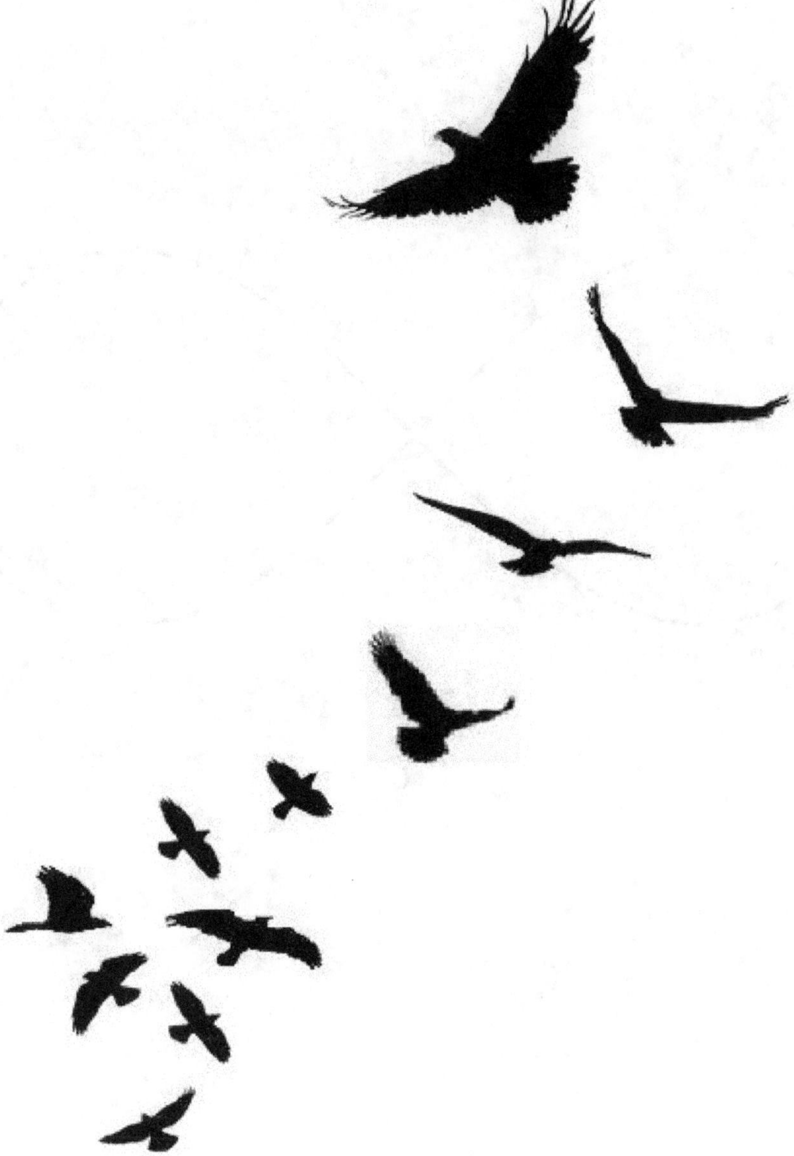

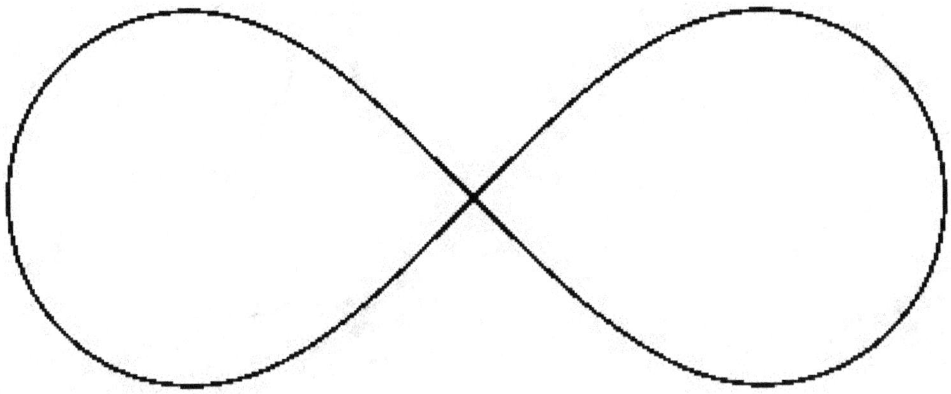

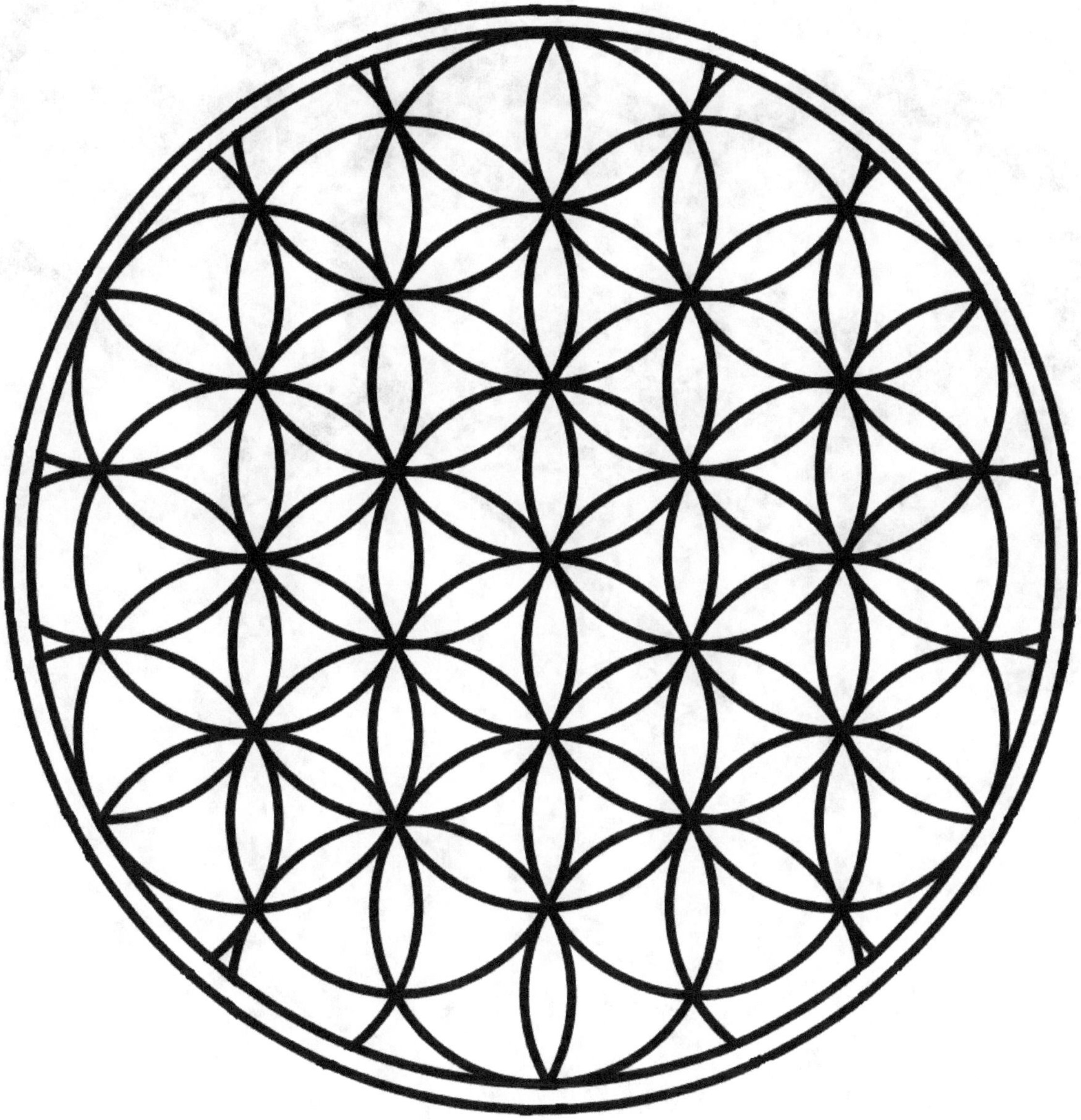

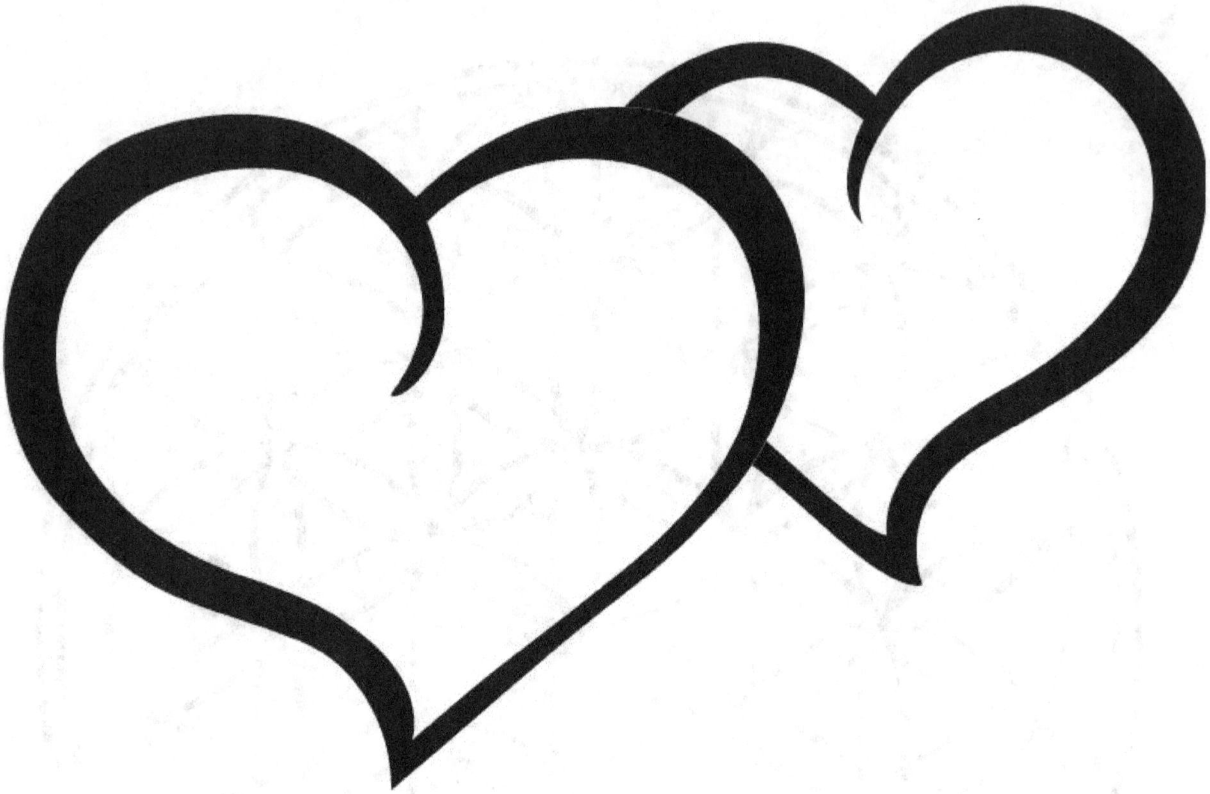

www.ingramcontent.com/pod-product-compliance
Lightning Source LLC
Chambersburg PA
CBHW081614220526
45468CB00010B/2866
9781981566891